KIDS' FAVORITES

CONTENTS

— PIANO LEVEL —
ELEMENTARY
(HLSPL LEVEL 2-3)

ISBN 978-0-634-03973-7

7777 W. BLUEMOUND RD. P.O. BOX 13819 MILWAUKEE, WI 53213

Visit Hal Leonard Online at
www.halleonard.com

PREFACE

The melodies in this collection have been kids' favorites for generations. I can remember enjoying many of these songs when I was a kid (yes, Lindsay and Sean, I was once a kid, too!) I had even more fun hearing them again when my children were little. God willing, I'll have the chance to share them with my grandchildren someday!

It is uniquely satisfying to play songs we know and love at the piano. I hope you have many happy hours together with these wonderful tunes.

This book is dedicated to my children, Lindsay Kay and Sean David. May you always retain the simple joys of childhood!

Sincerely,
Phillip Keveren

BIOGRAPHY

Phillip Keveren, a multi-talented keyboard artist and composer, has composed original works in a variety of genres from piano solo to symphonic orchestra. Mr. Keveren gives frequent concerts and workshops for teachers and their students in the United States, Canada, Europe, and Asia. Mr. Keveren holds a B.M. in composition from California State University Northridge and a M.M. in composition from the University of Southern California.

ALOUETTE

French Folksong
Arranged by Phillip Keveren

Gently

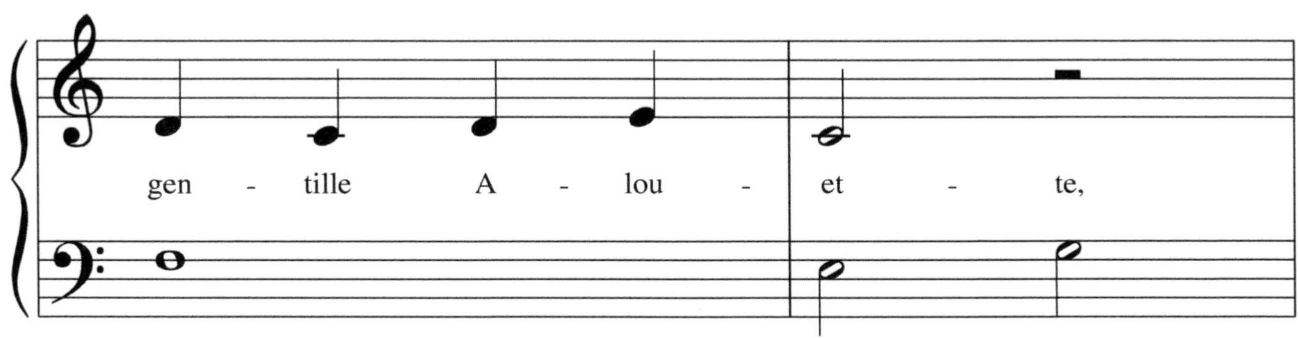

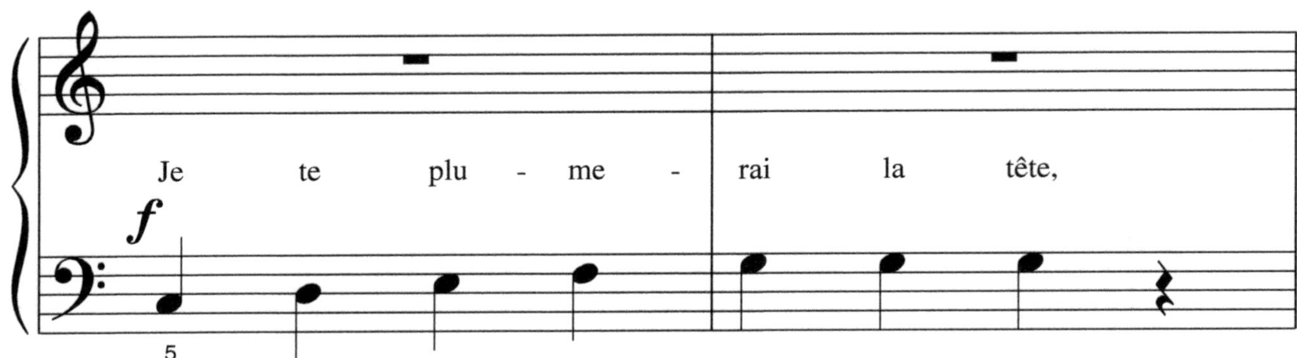
Je te plu - me - rai la tête,
f
5

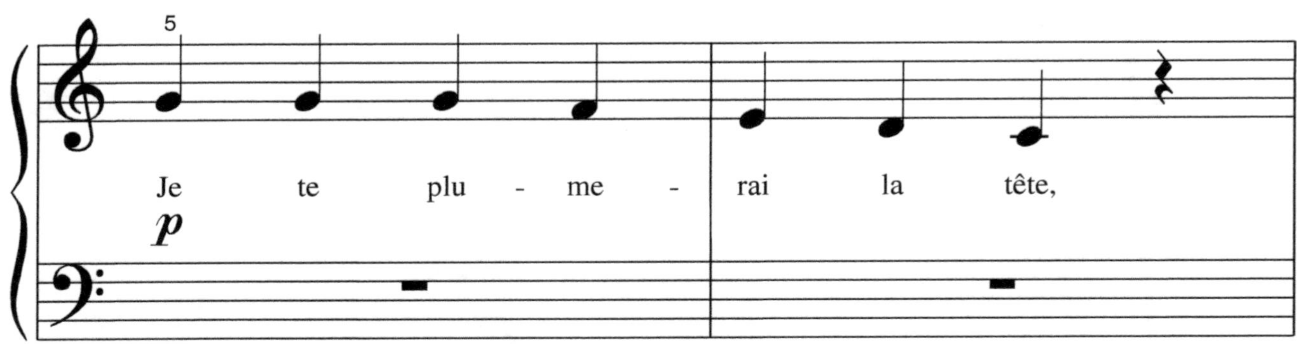
5
Je te plu - me - rai la tête,
p

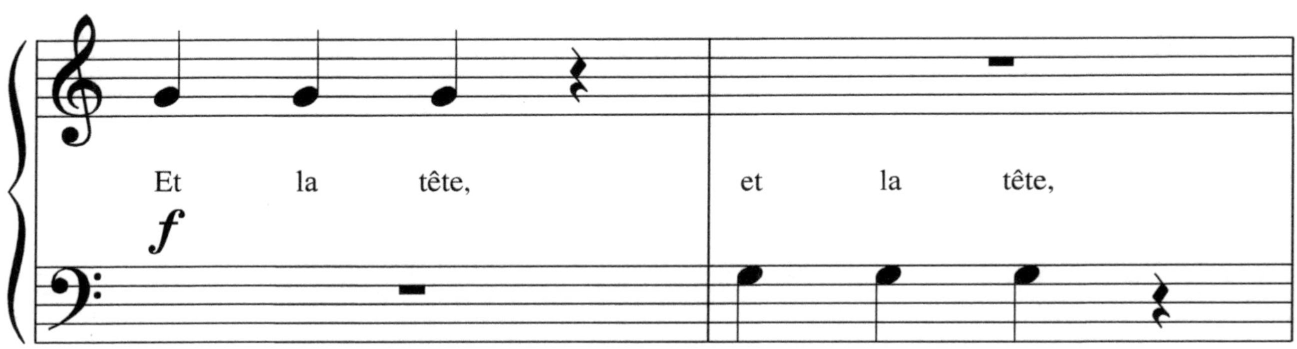
Et la tête, et la tête,
f

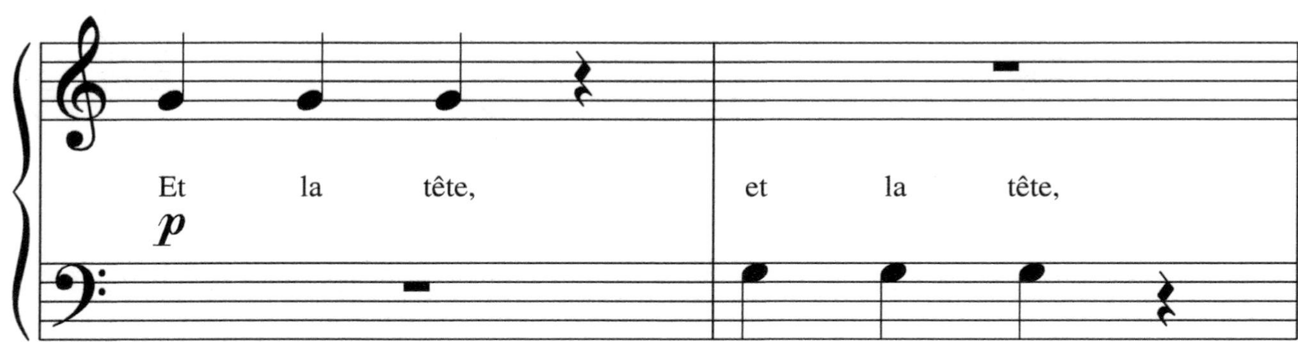
Et la tête, et la tête,
p

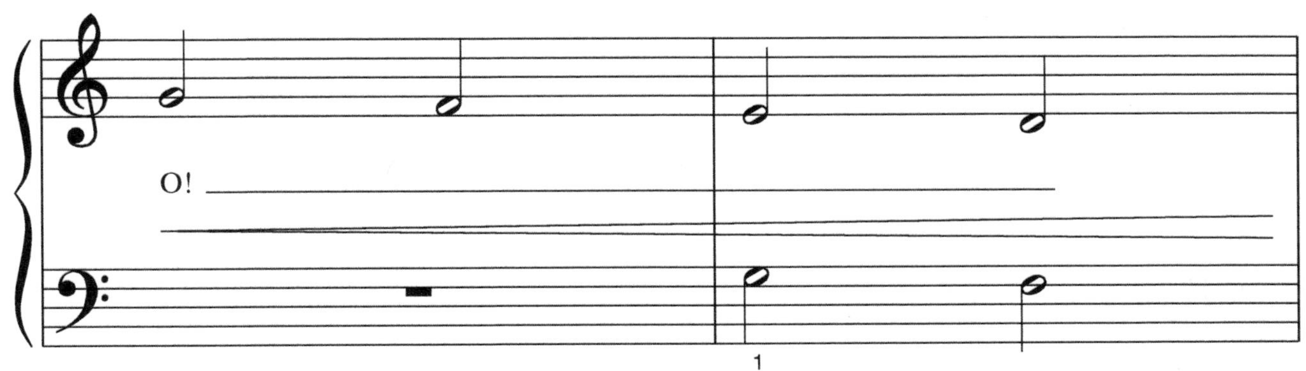
O!
1

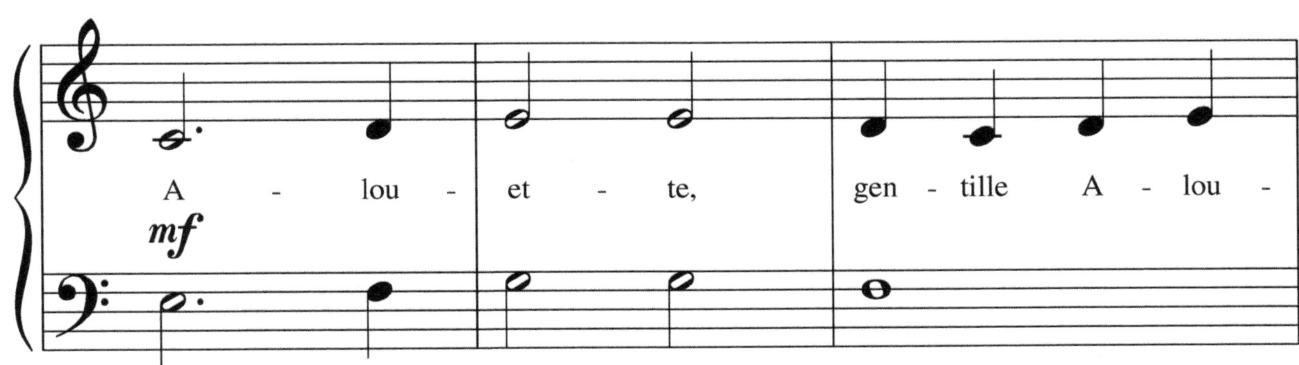
A - lou - et - te, gen - tille A - lou -
mf

et - te, A - lou - et - te,

je te plu - me - rai.
rit.

A-TISKET A-TASKET

Traditional
Arranged by Phillip Keveren

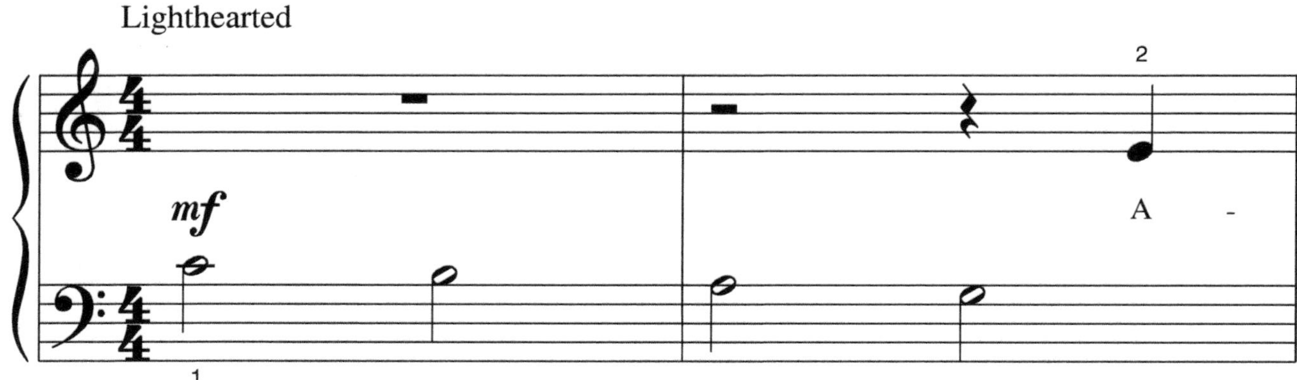

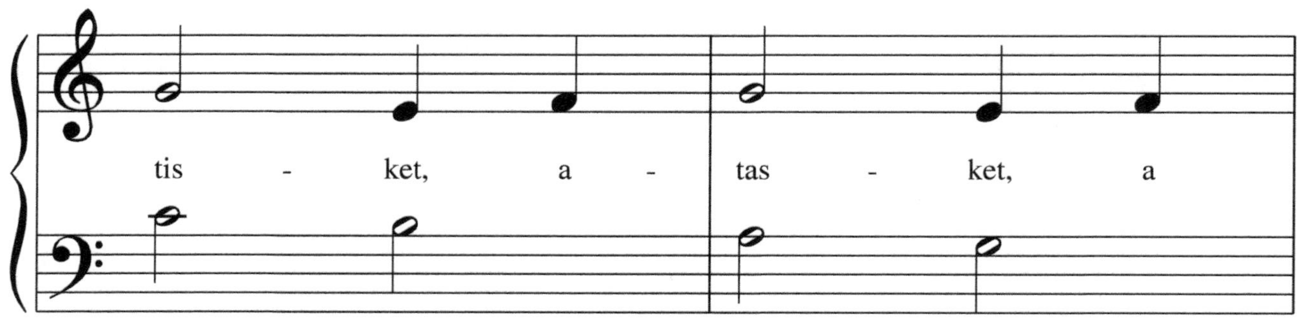

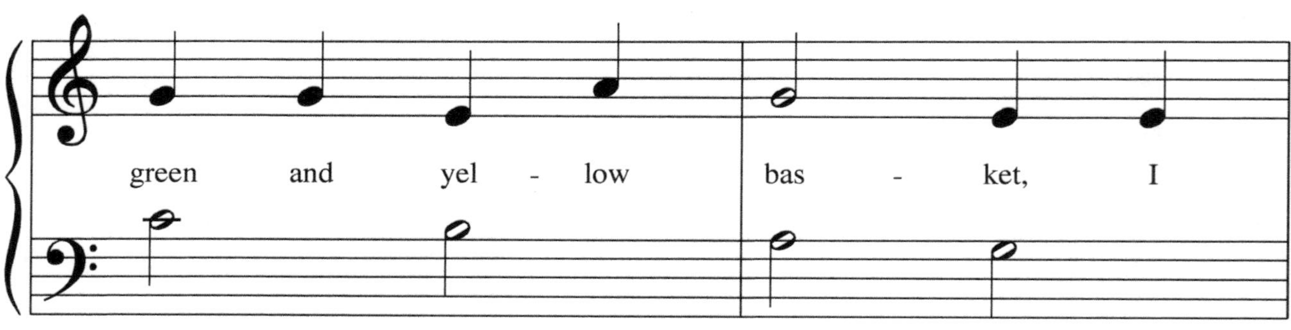

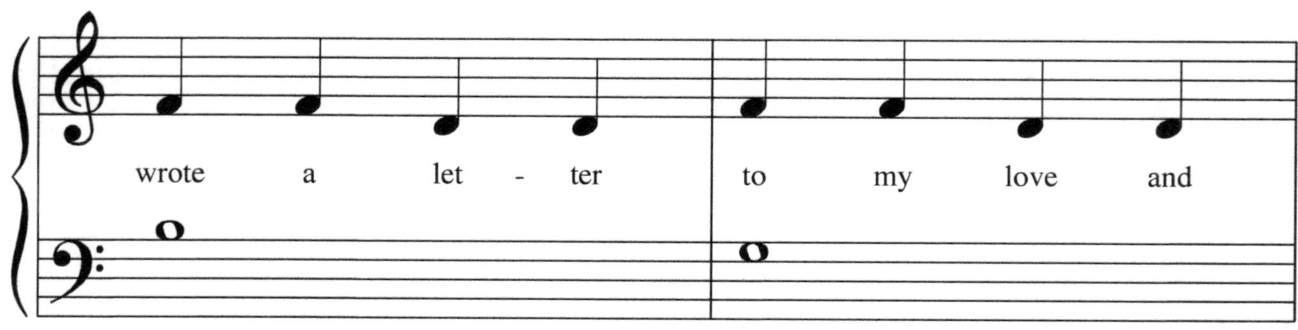

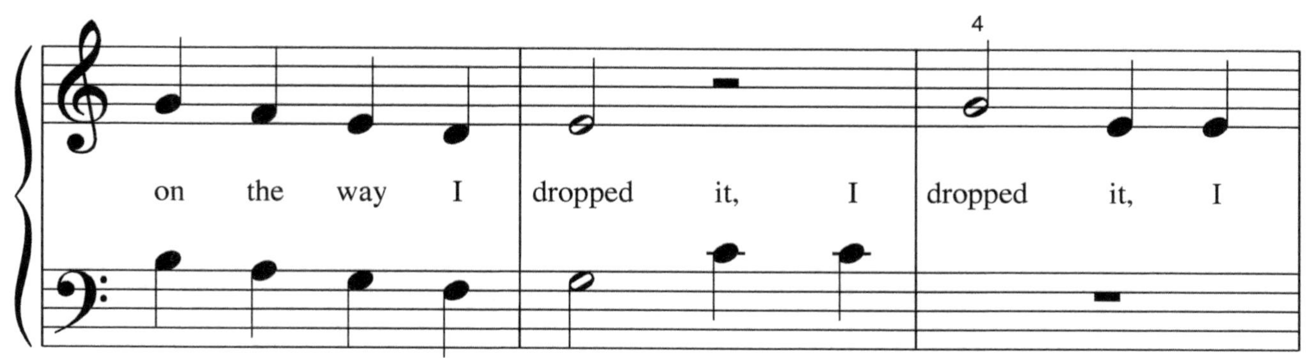
4
on the way I
dropped it, I
dropped it, I

dropped it, and
on the way I
dropped it, A
1

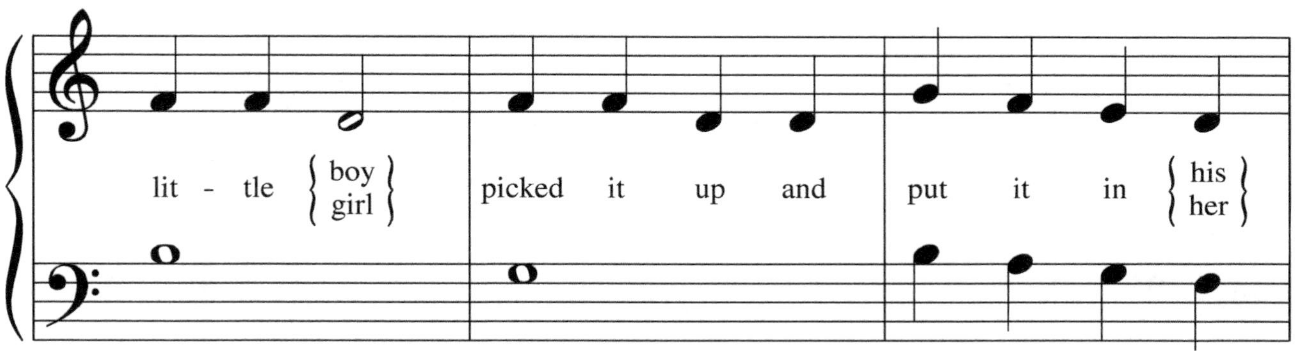
lit - tle
boy
girl
picked it up and
put it in
his
her

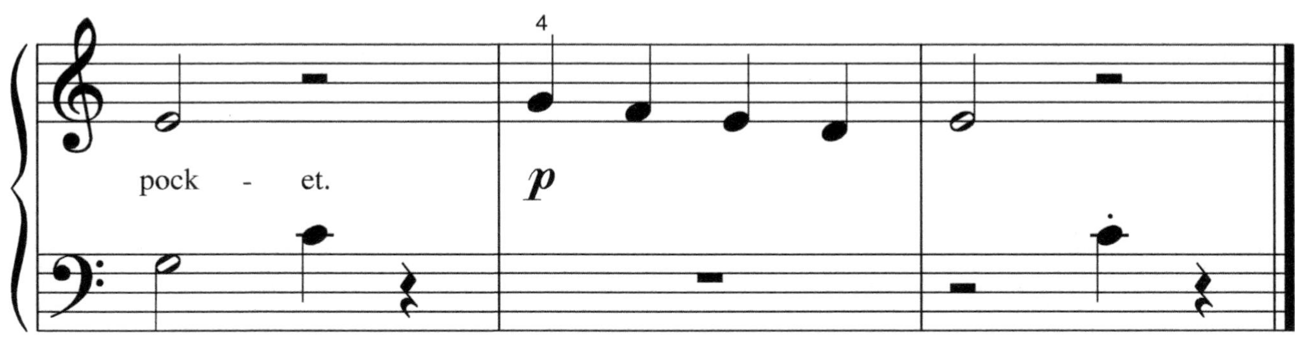
pock - et.
4
p

ALPHABET SONG

Traditional American School Song
Arranged by Phillip Keveren

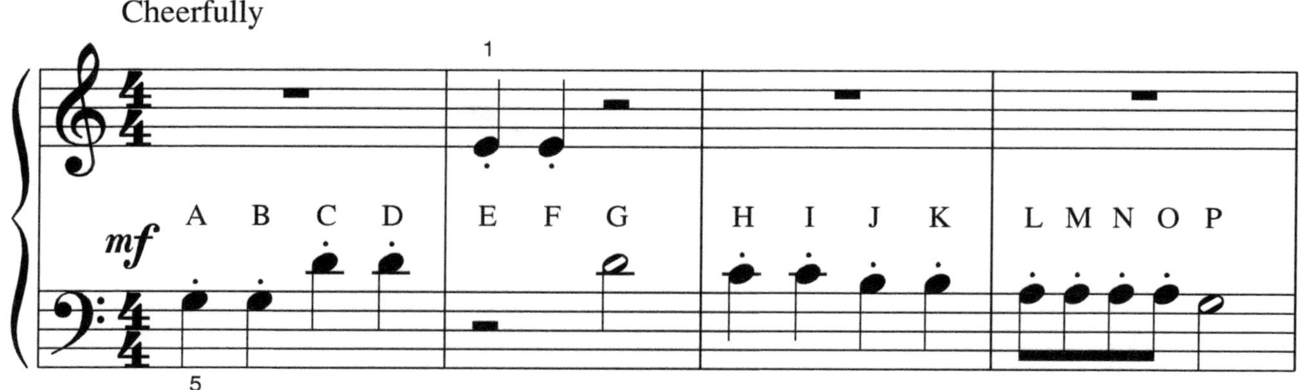

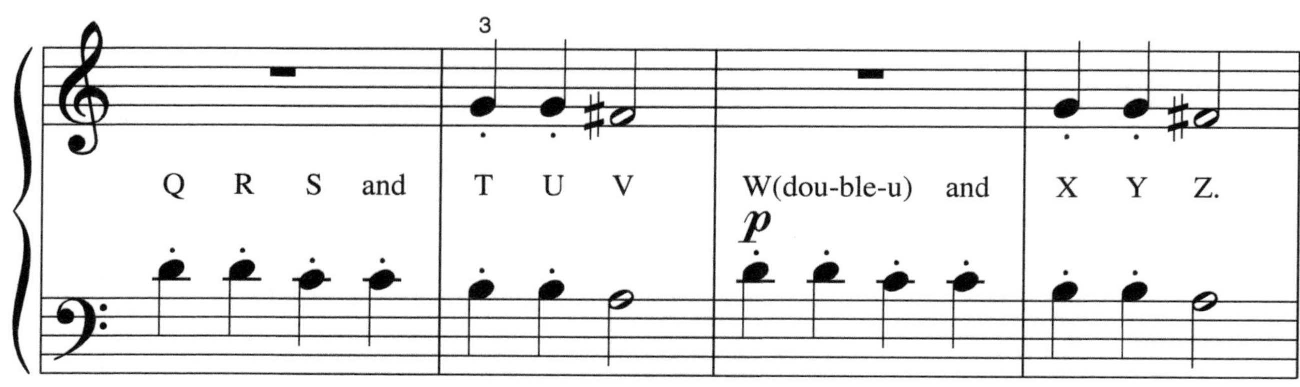

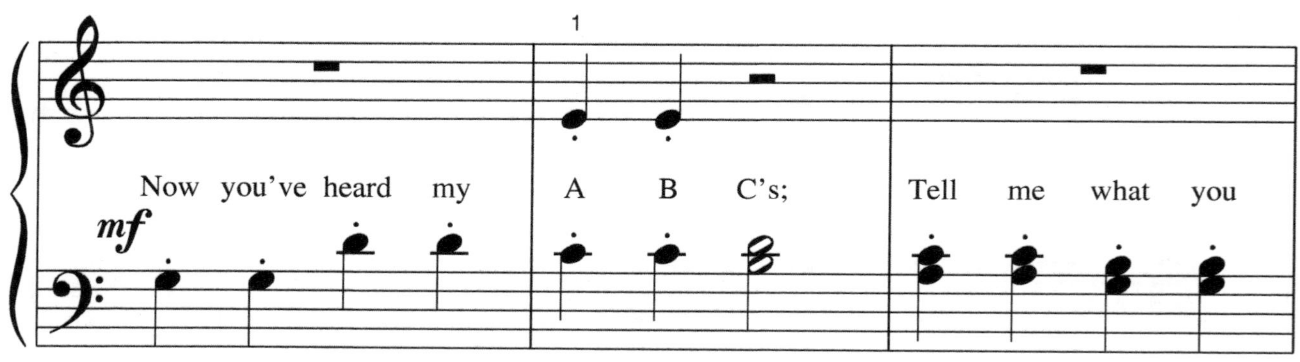

THE BEAR WENT OVER THE MOUNTAIN

Traditional American
Arranged by Phillip Keveren

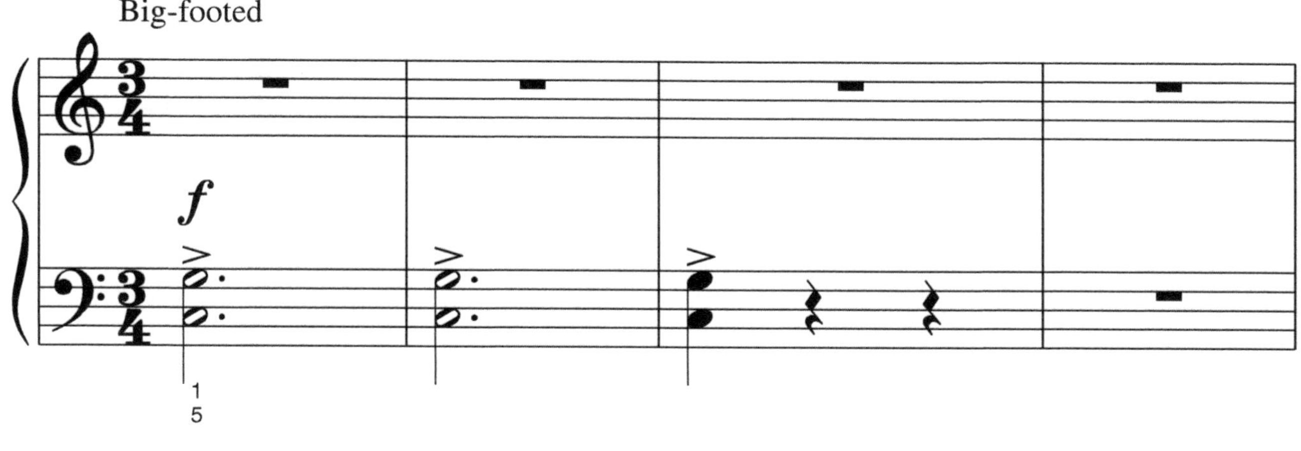

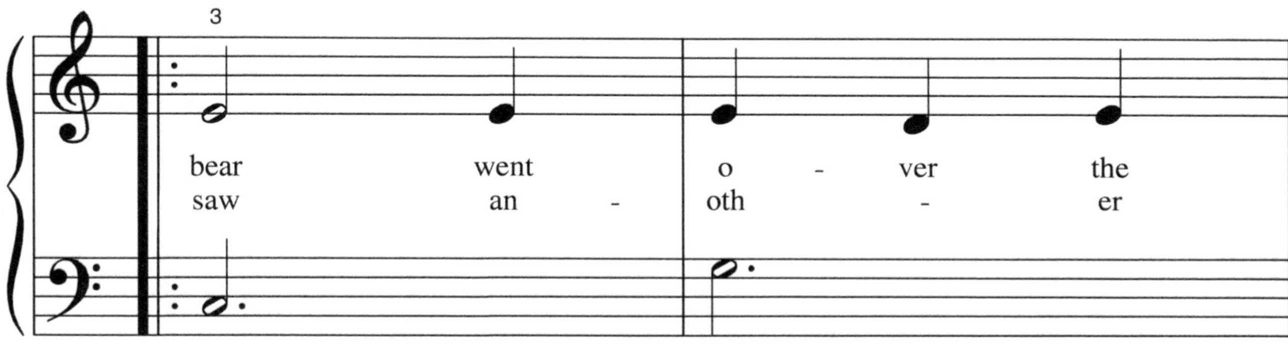

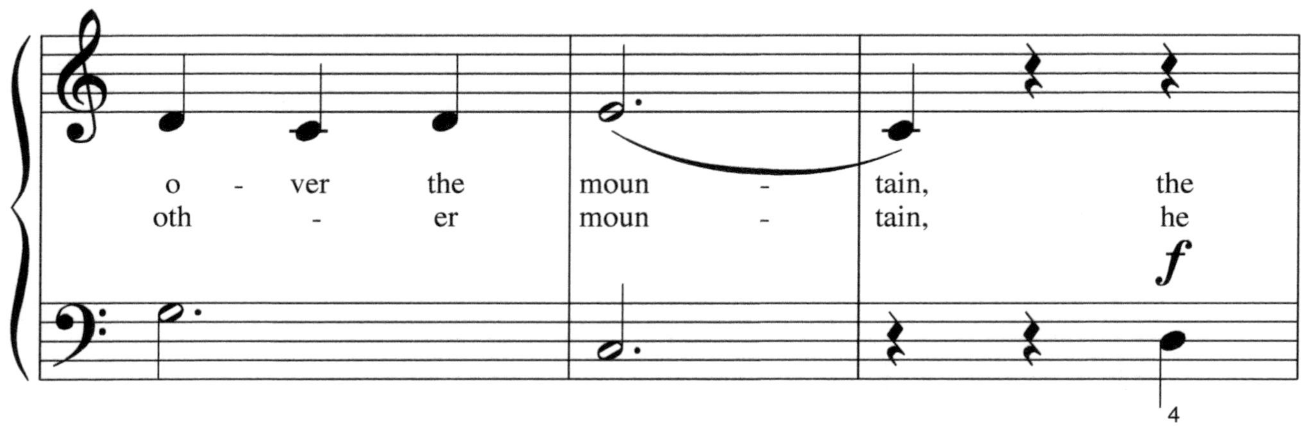
o - ver the moun - tain, the
oth - er moun - tain, he
f
4

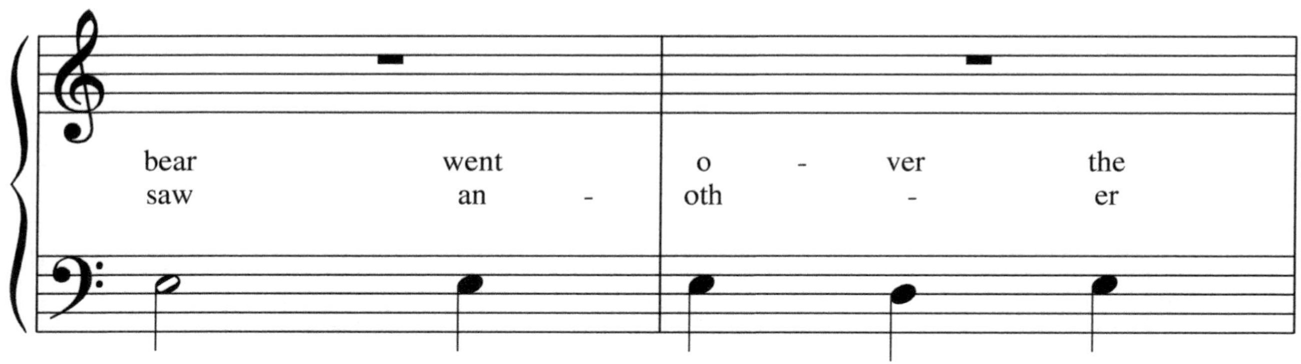
bear went o - ver the
saw an - oth - er

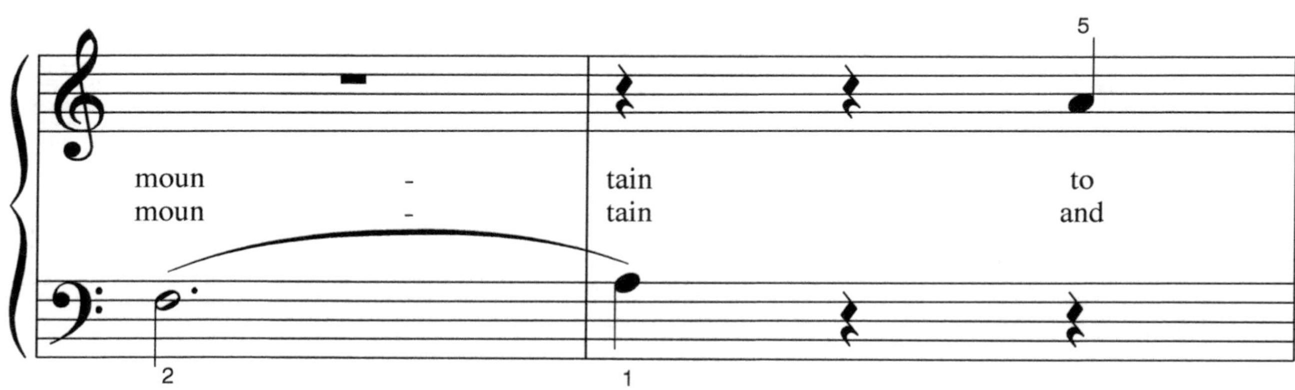
5
moun - tain to
moun - tain and
2
1

4 3 2 1
see what he could see.
that's what he could see.
1
5

1.
2.
5
1
He
mf

BE KIND TO YOUR WEB-FOOTED FRIENDS

Traditional Words
Music from "The Stars and Stripes Forever"
by JOHN PHILIP SOUSA
Arranged by Phillip Keveren

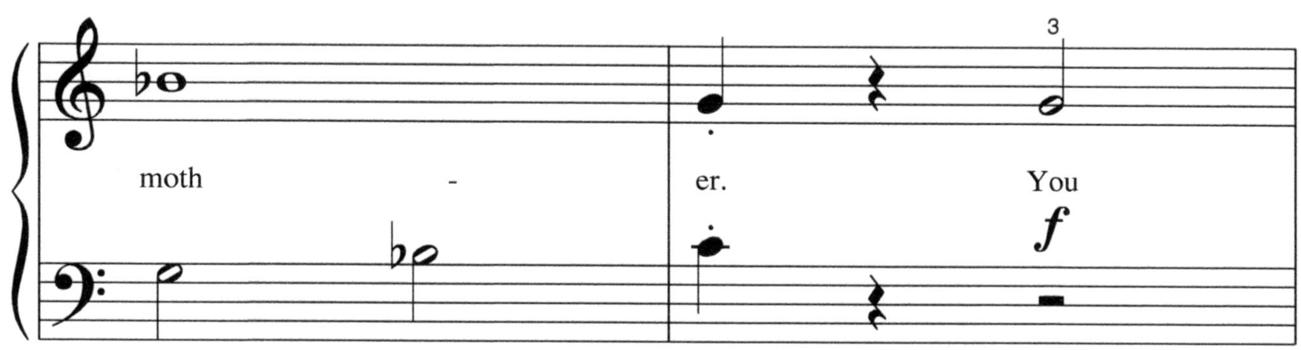
3
moth - er. You
f

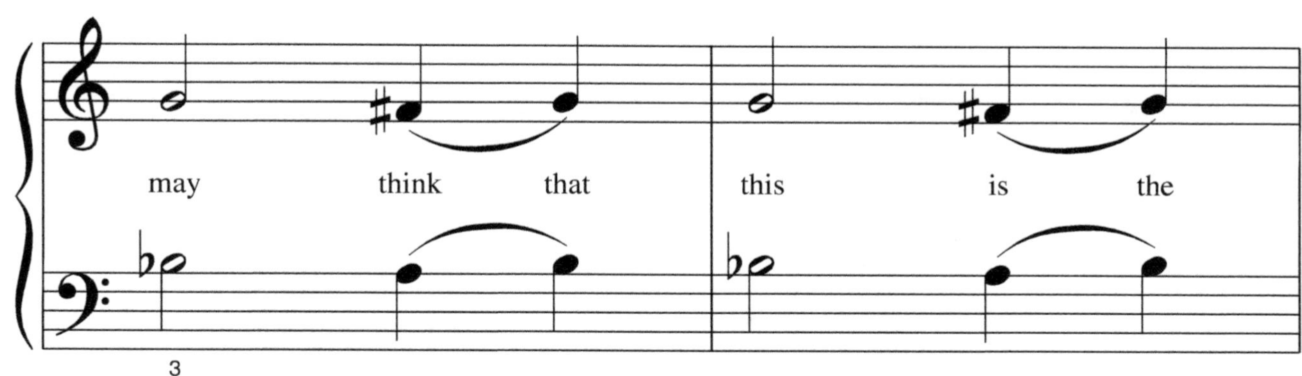
may think that this is the
3

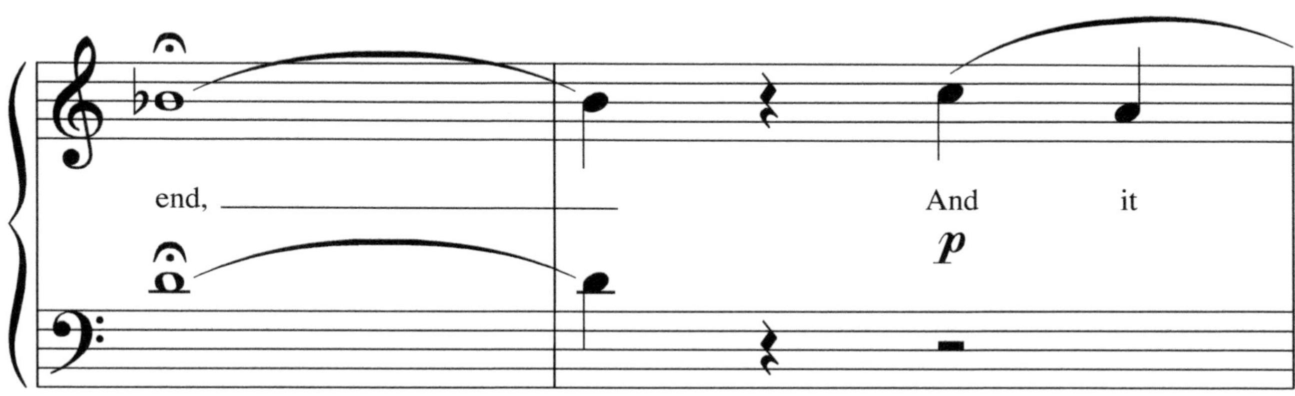
end, And it
p

is!
pp
1

DOWN BY THE STATION

Traditional
Arranged by Phillip Keveren

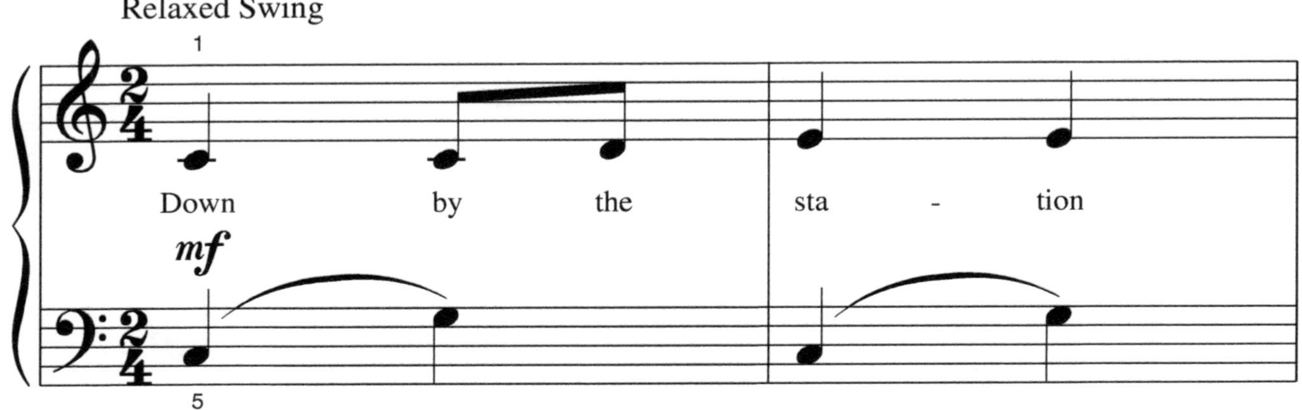

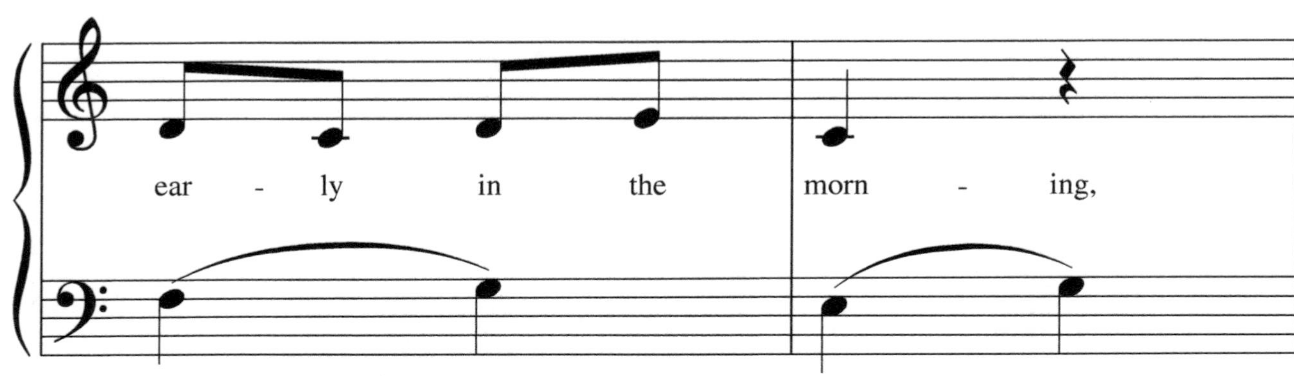

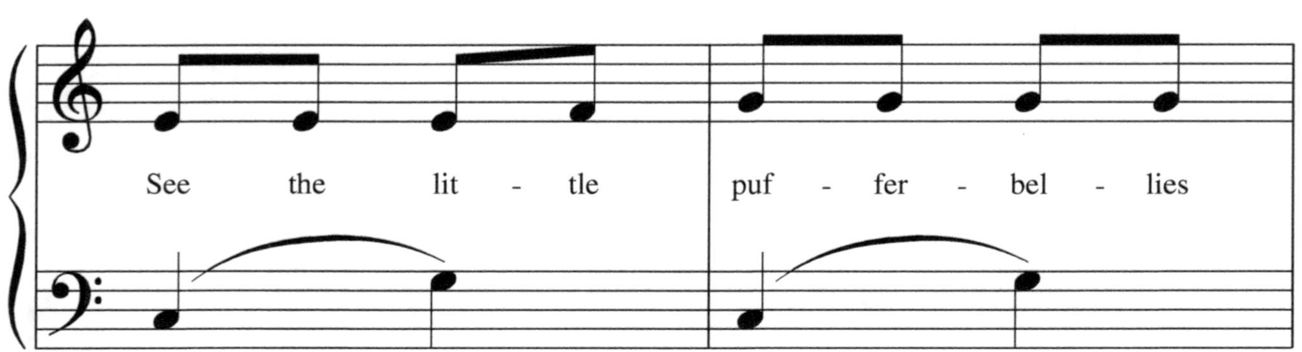

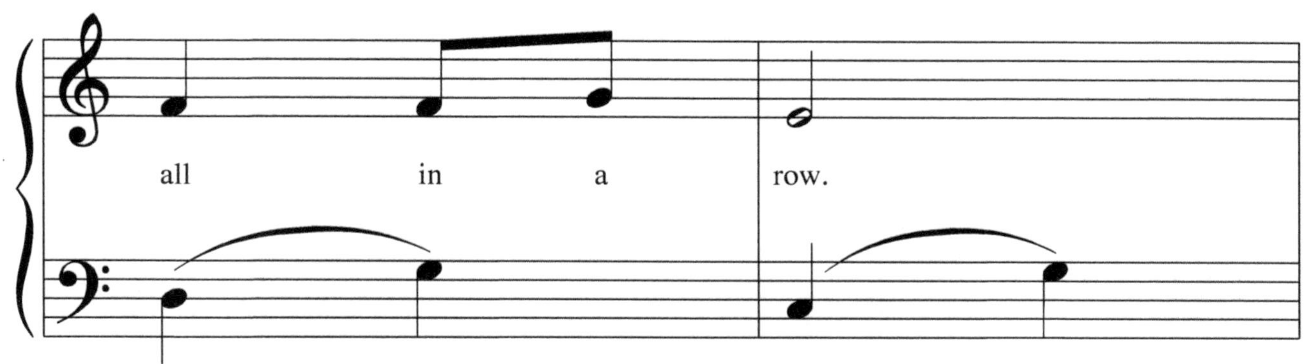
all in a row.

See the en - gine driv - er

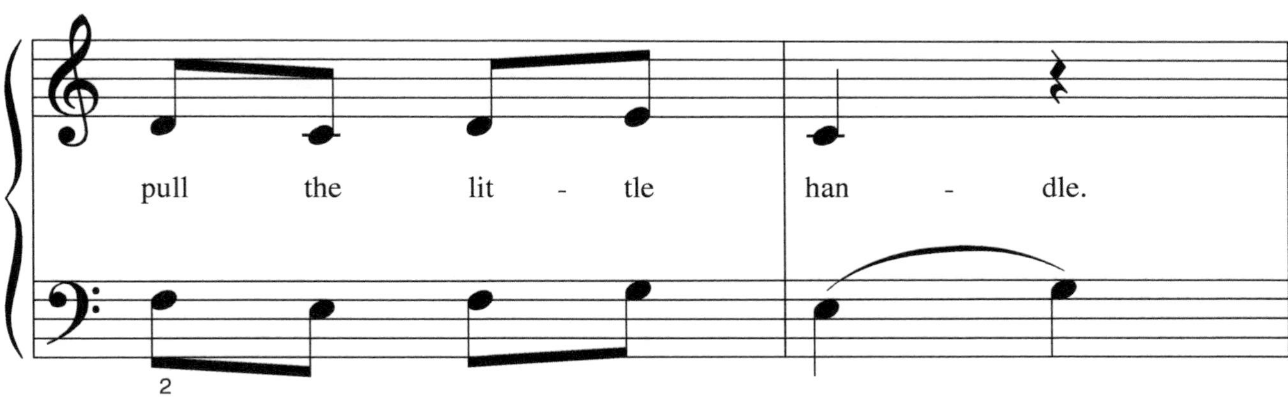
pull the lit - tle han - dle.
2

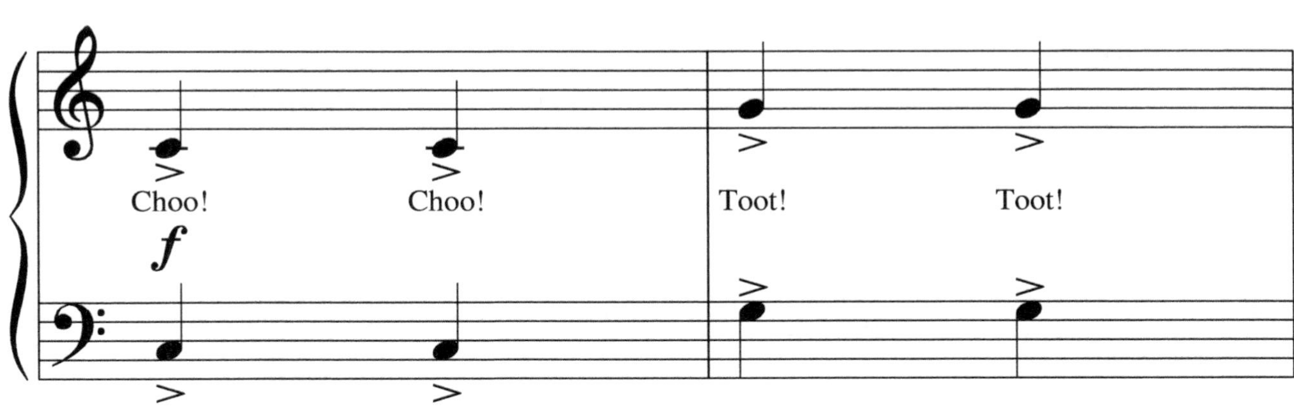
Choo! Choo! Toot! Toot!
f

off
they
go!
mf
5
2
1
2
8vb
mp
(8vb)
p
rit.
5
3
1
pp
(8vb)

FRÈRE JACQUES
(Are You Sleeping?)

Traditional French Song
Arranged by Phillip Keveren

Slowly

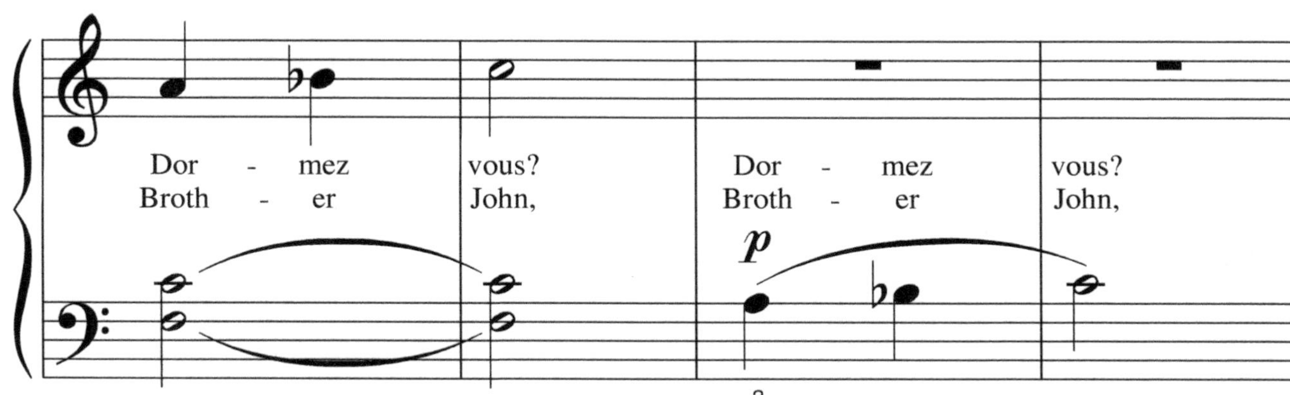

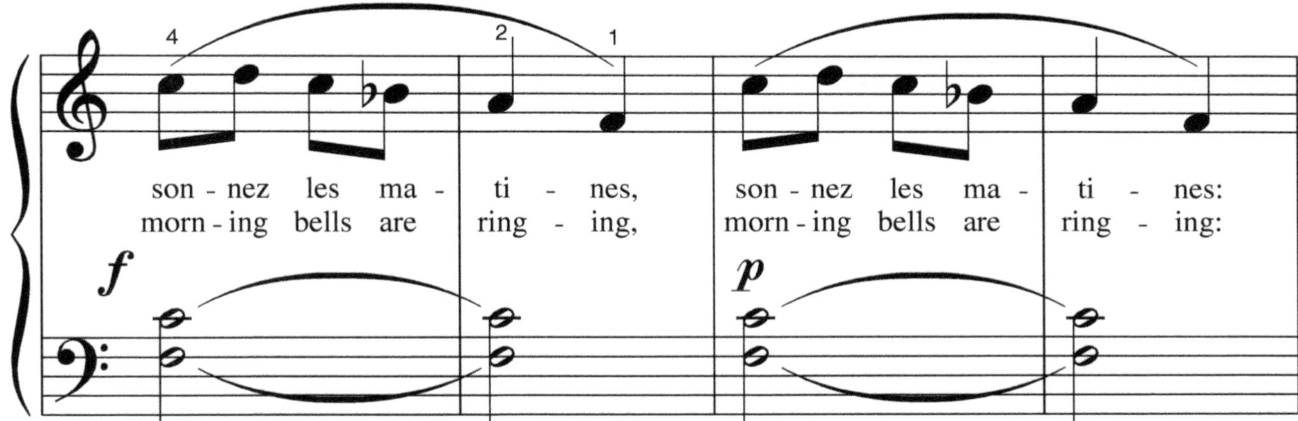

EENSY, WEENSY SPIDER

North Carolina Children's Song
Arranged by Phillip Keveren

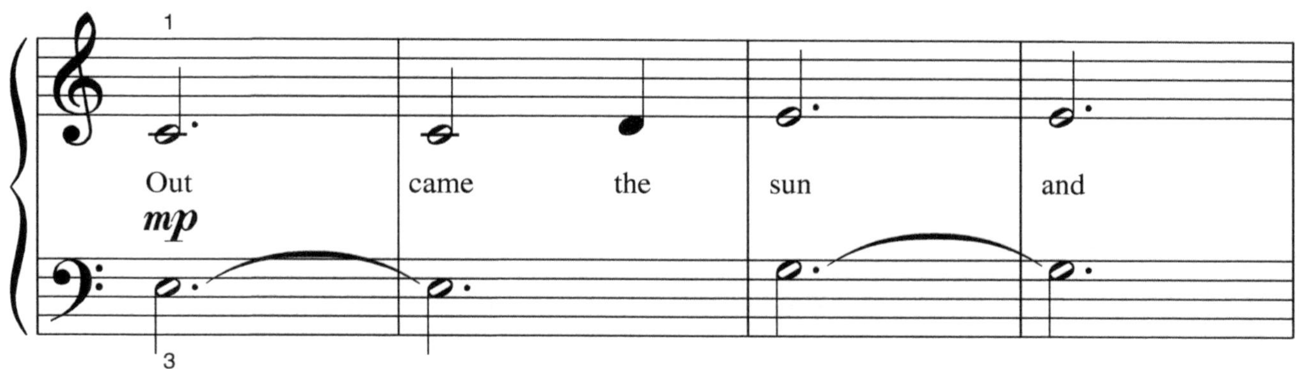
1
Out came the sun and
mp
3

dried up all the rain, And the

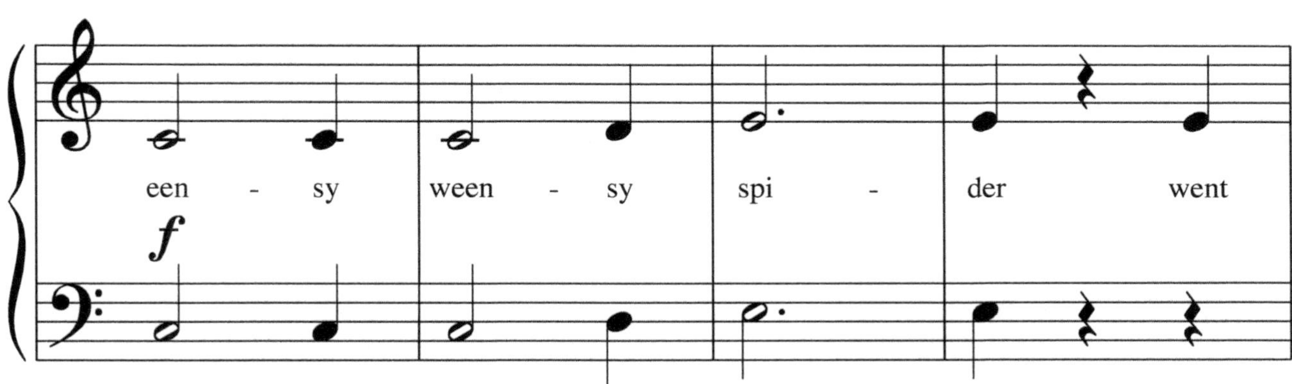
een - sy ween - sy spi - der went
f

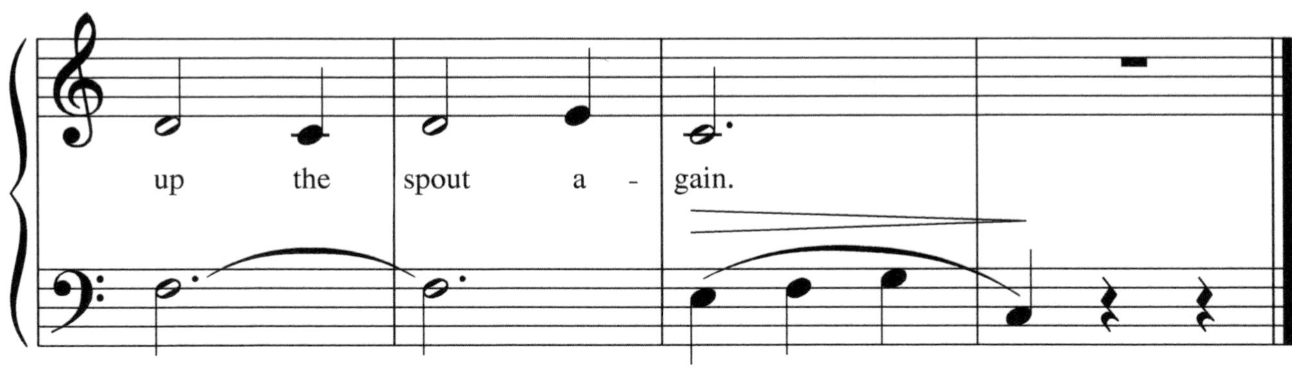
up the spout a - gain.

GIT ALONG, LITTLE DOGIES

Western American Cowboy Song
Arranged by Phillip Keveren

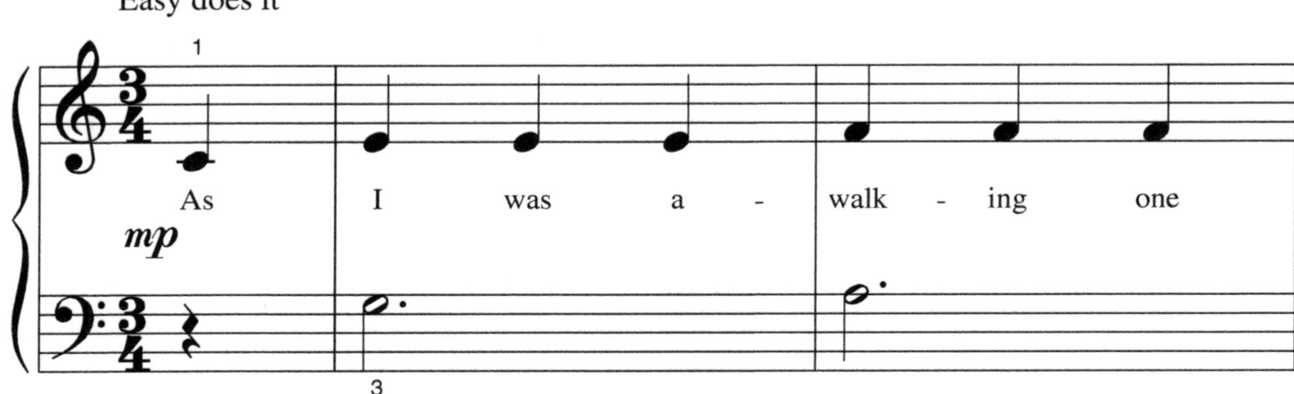

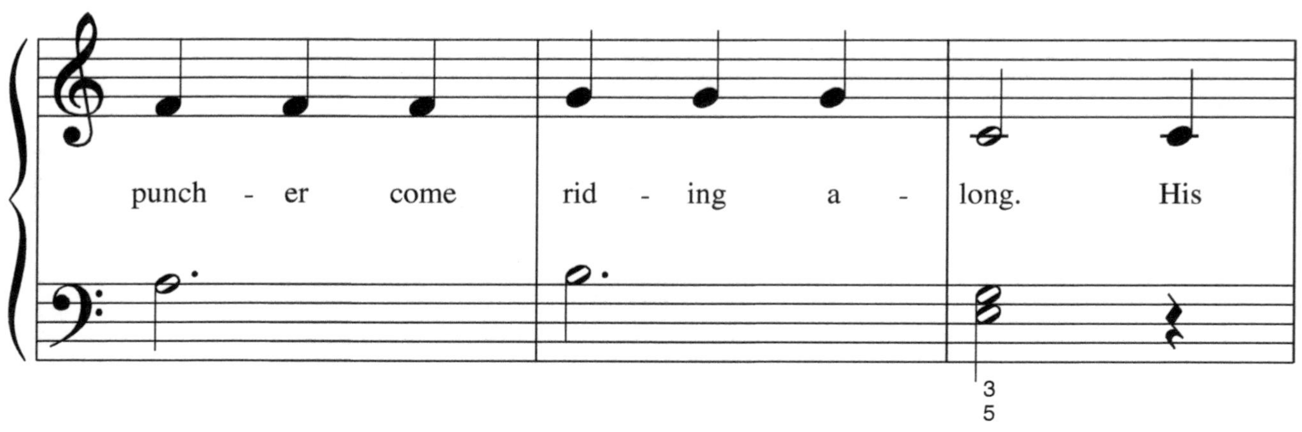

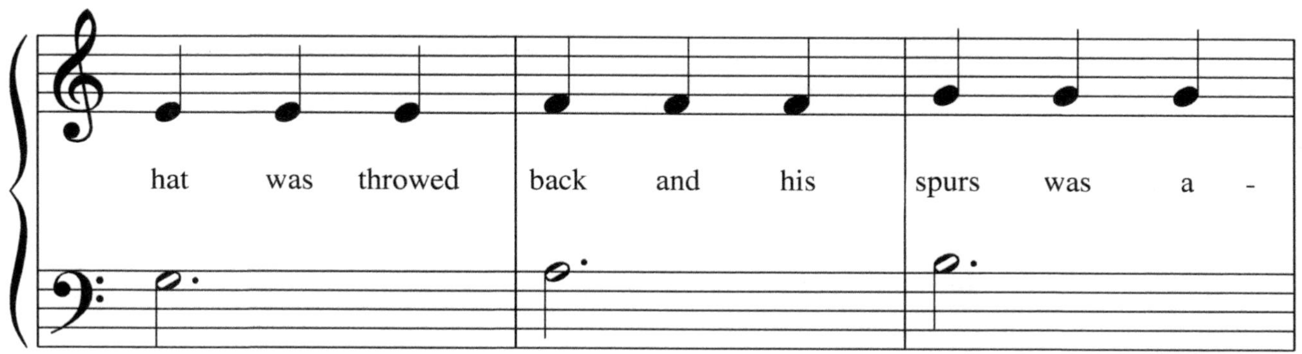
hat was throwed back and his spurs was a -

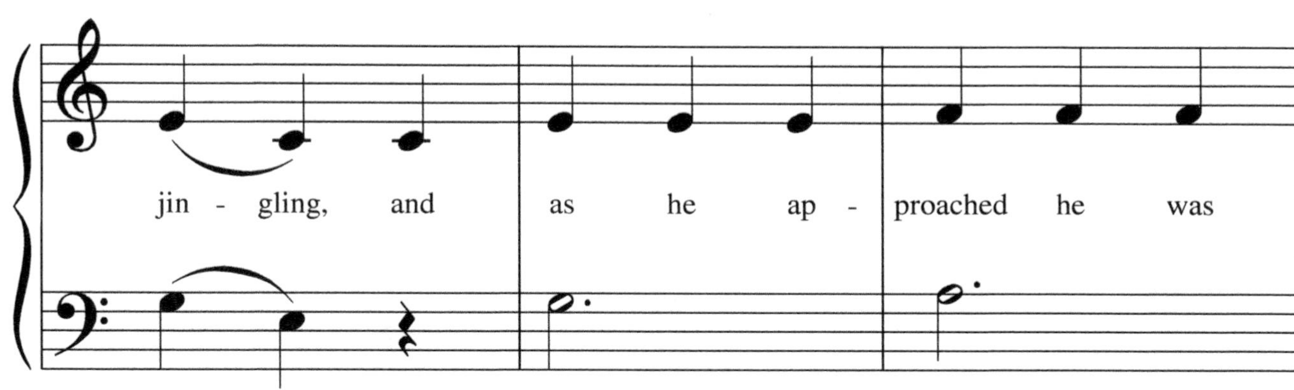
jin - gling, and as he ap - proached he was

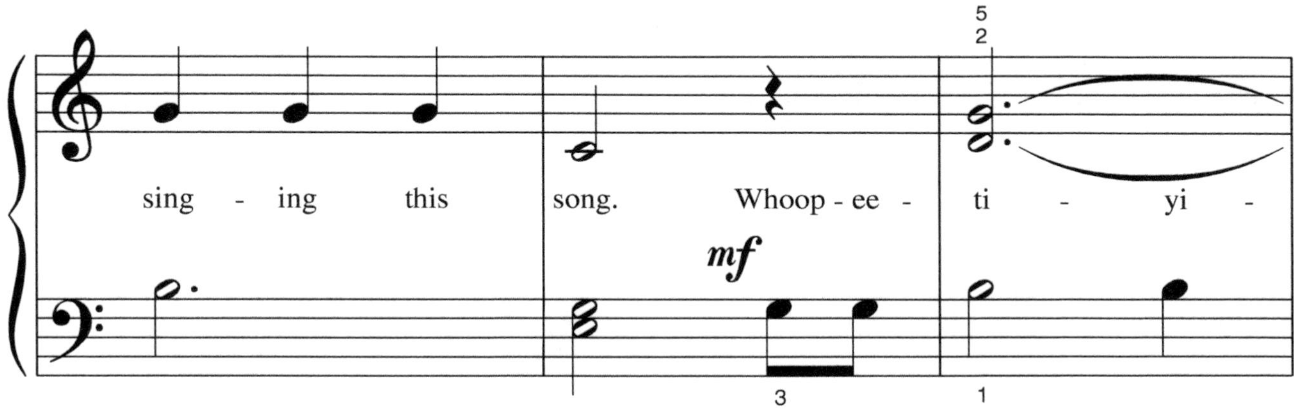
sing - ing this song. Whoop - ee - ti - yi -
mf

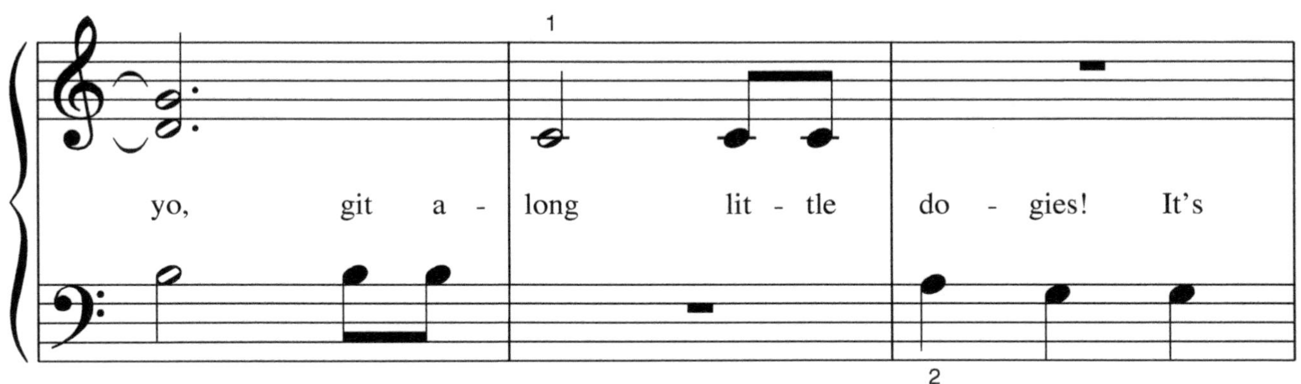
yo, git a - long lit - tle do - gies! It's

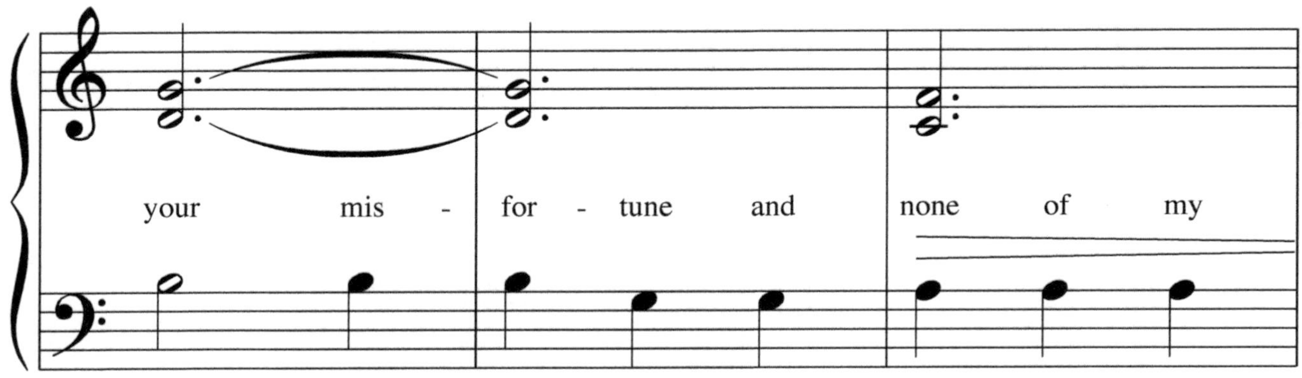
your mis - for - tune and none of my

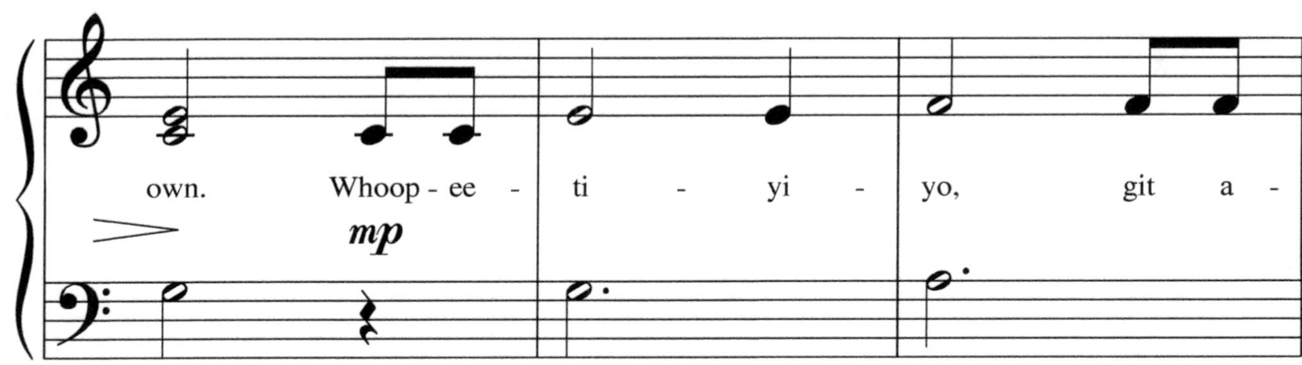
own. Whoop - ee - ti - yi - yo, git a -
mp

long, lit - tle do - gies! You know that Wy -

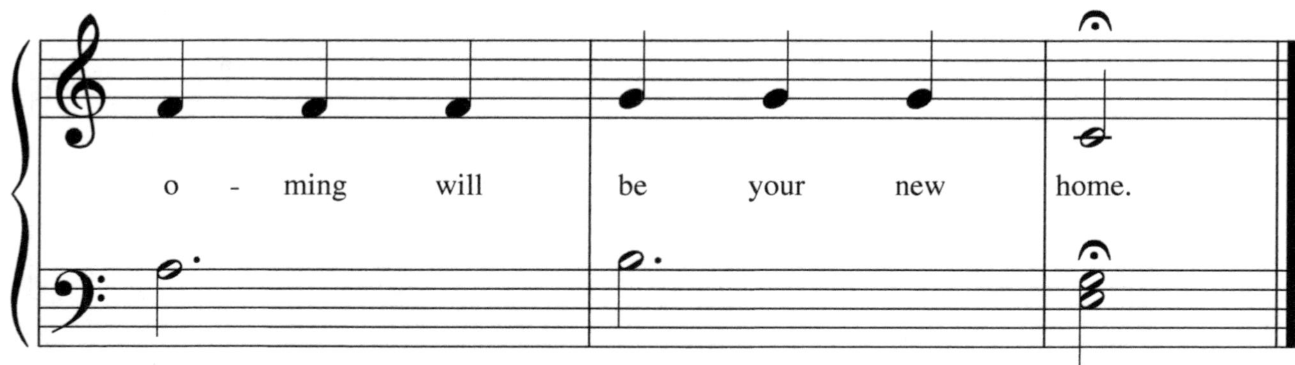
o - ming will be your new home.

GRANDFATHER'S CLOCK

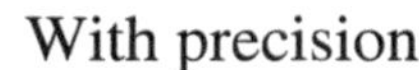

By HENRY CLAY WORK

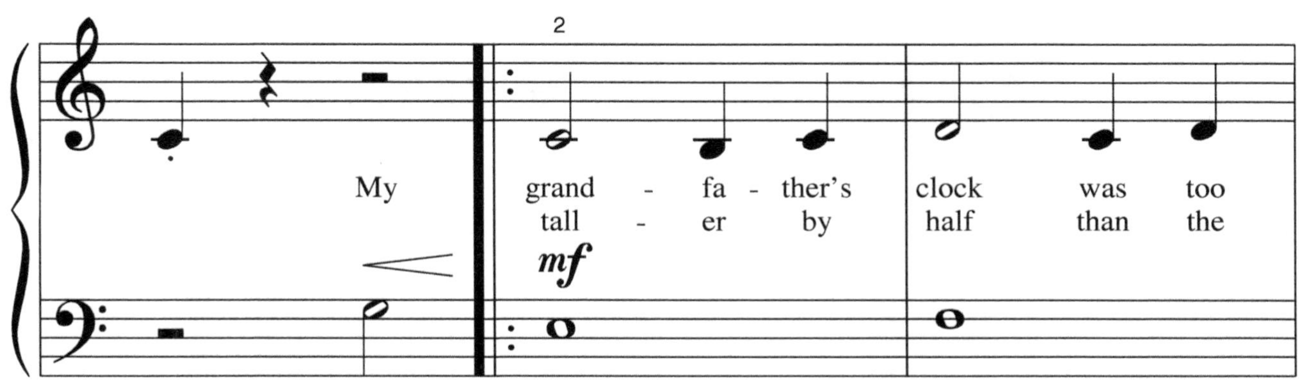

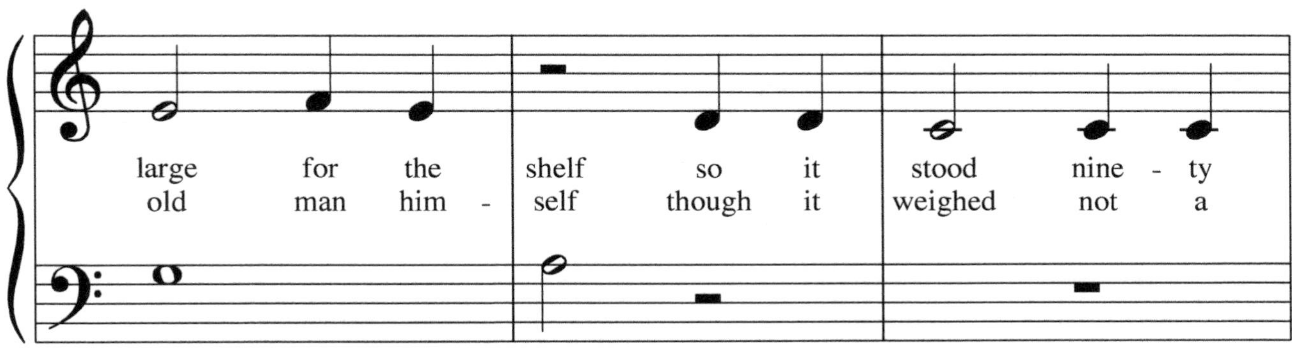

1.
2.
It was
It was
bought on the morn of the day that he was
born and was al - ways his treas - ure and
pride;
But it
stopped

short
never to go a - gain when the

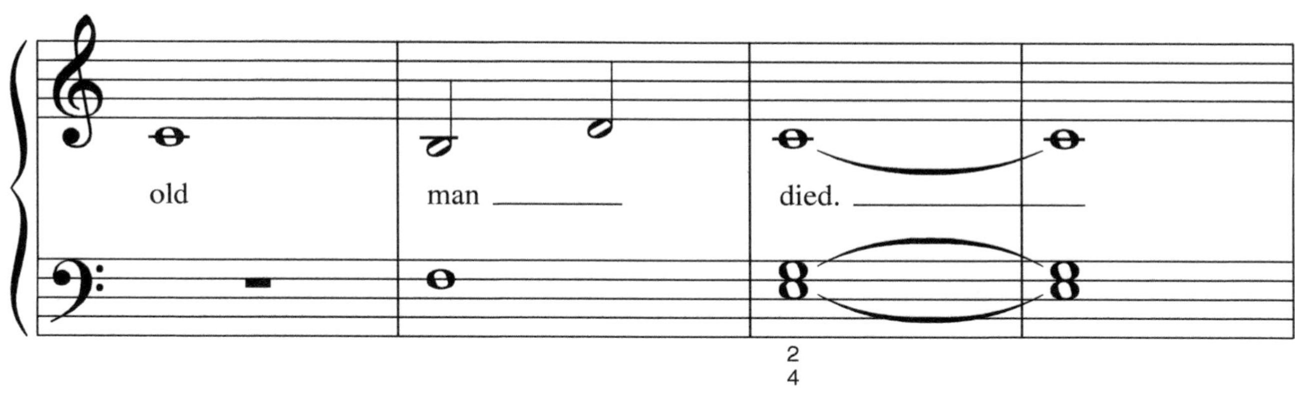
old
man
died.
2
4

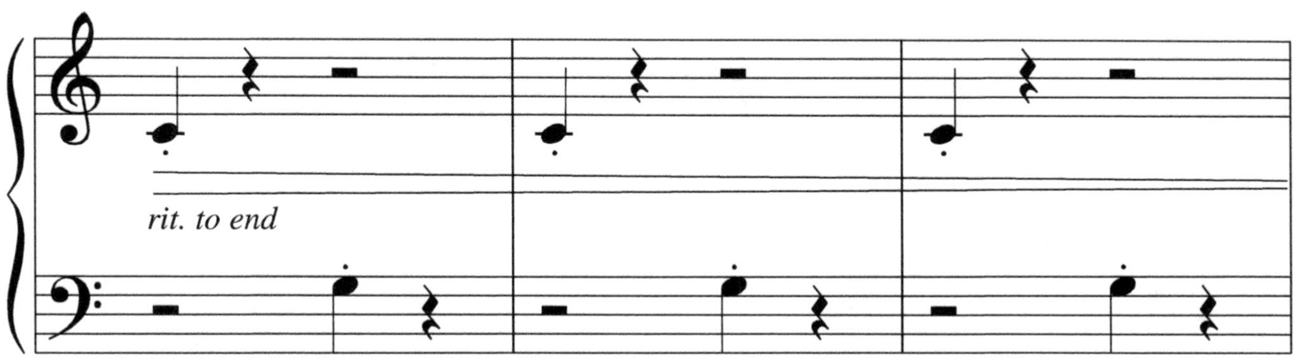
rit. to end

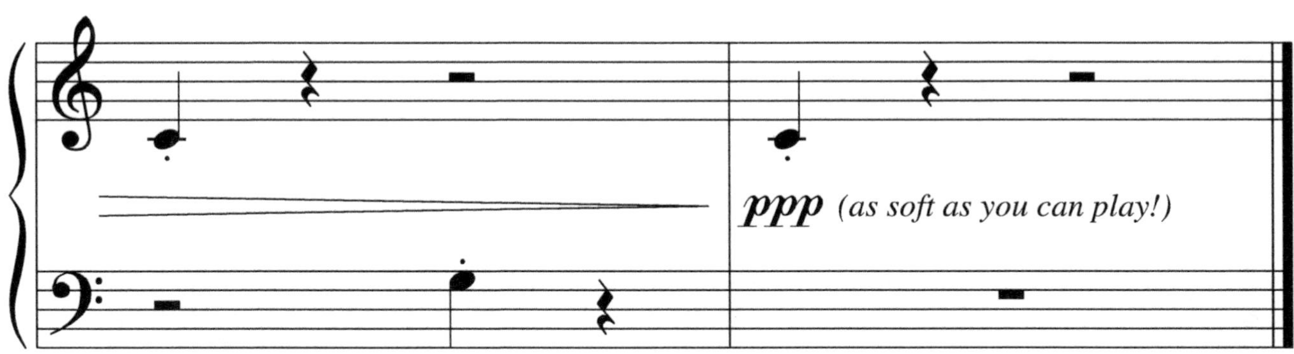
ppp (as soft as you can play!)

HICKORY DICKORY DOCK

Nursery Rhyme Song
Arranged by Phillip Keveren

HOME ON THE RANGE

Lyrics by DR. BREWSTER HIGLEY
Music by DAN KELLY
Arranged by Phillip Keveren

Warmly

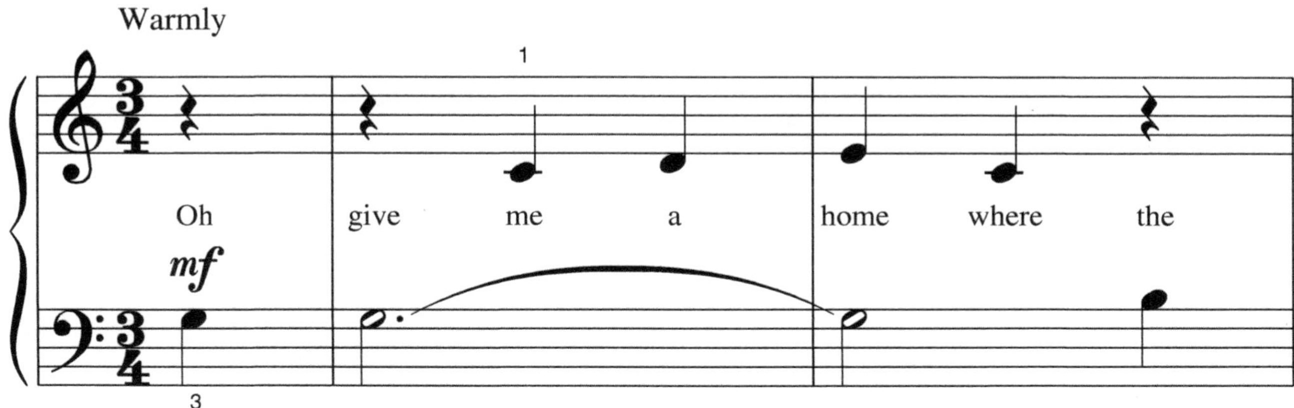

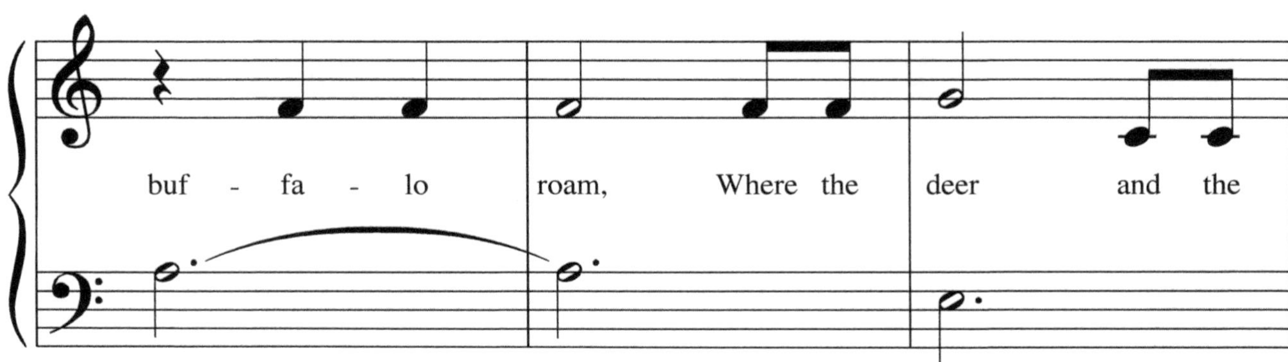

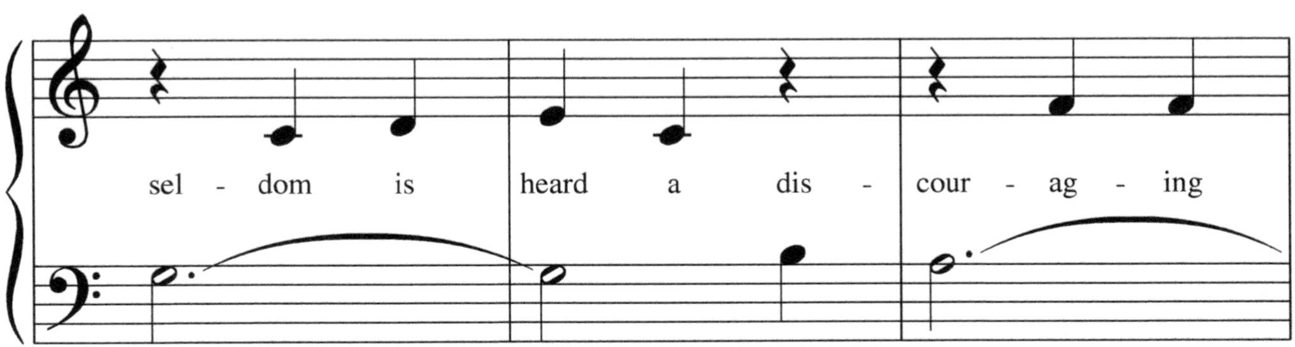

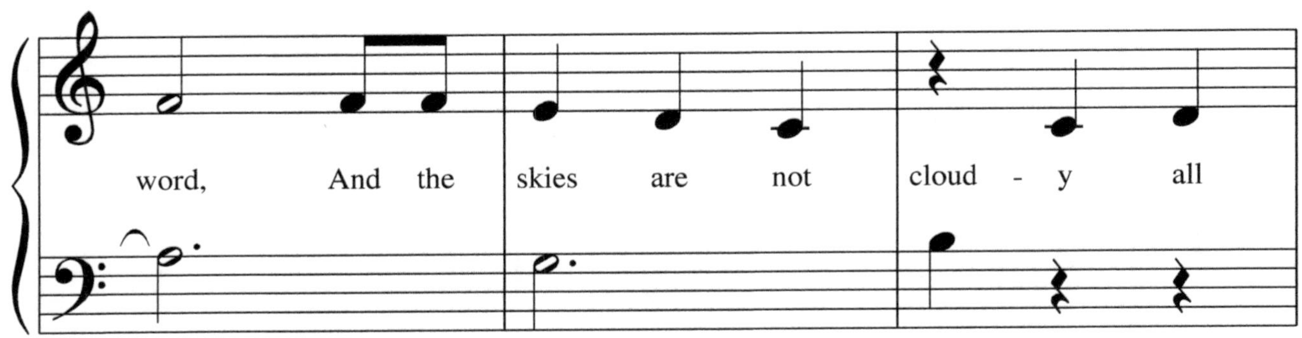
word, And the skies are not cloud - y all

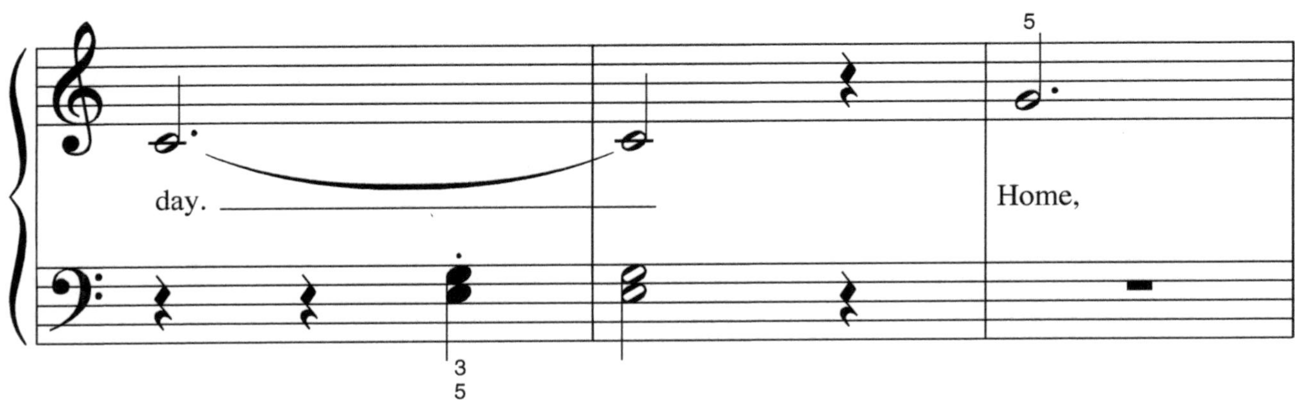
5
day.
Home,
3
5

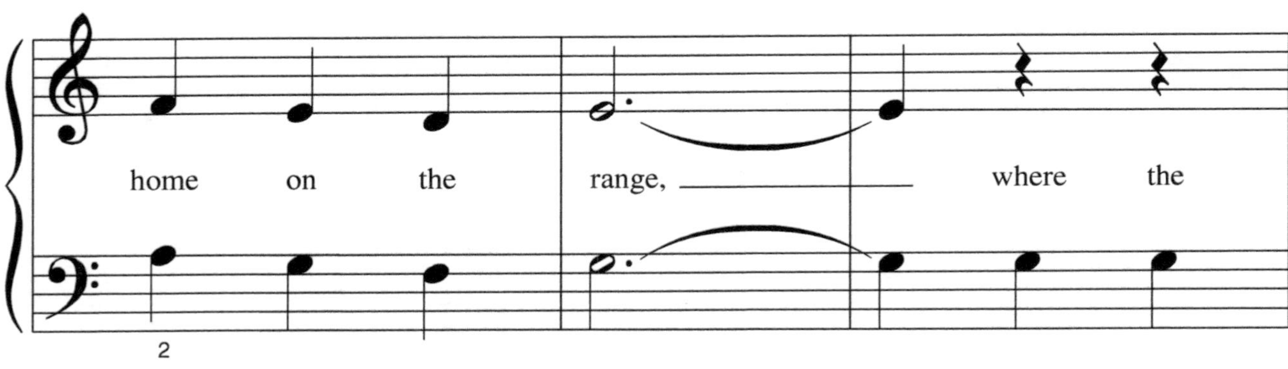
home on the range, where the
2

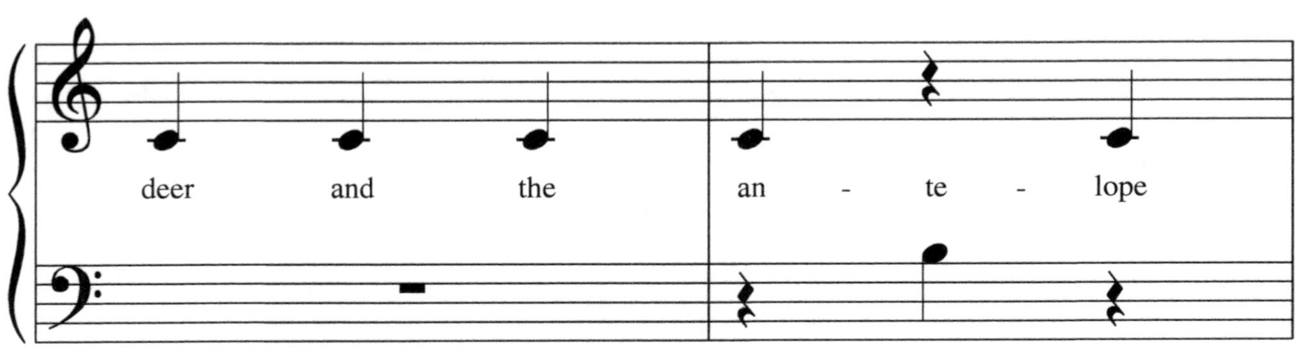
deer and the an - te - lope

play.
Where
sel - dom is

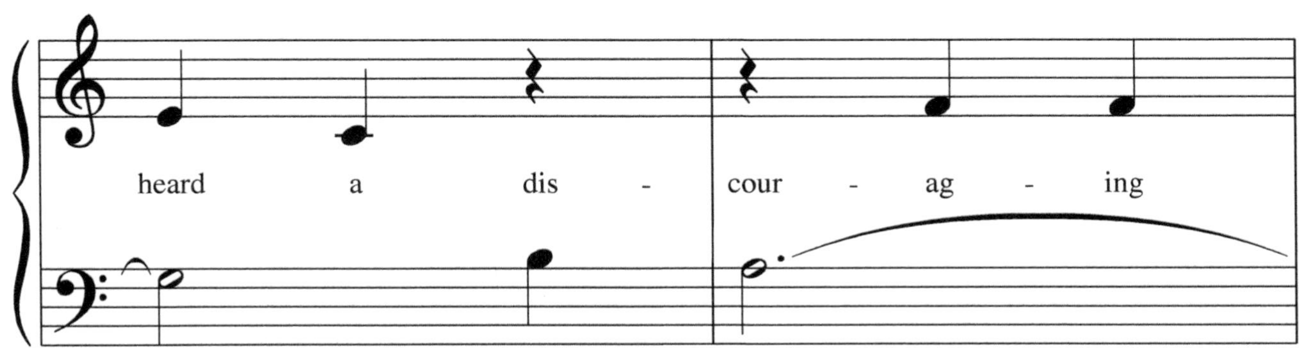
heard a dis -
cour - ag - ing

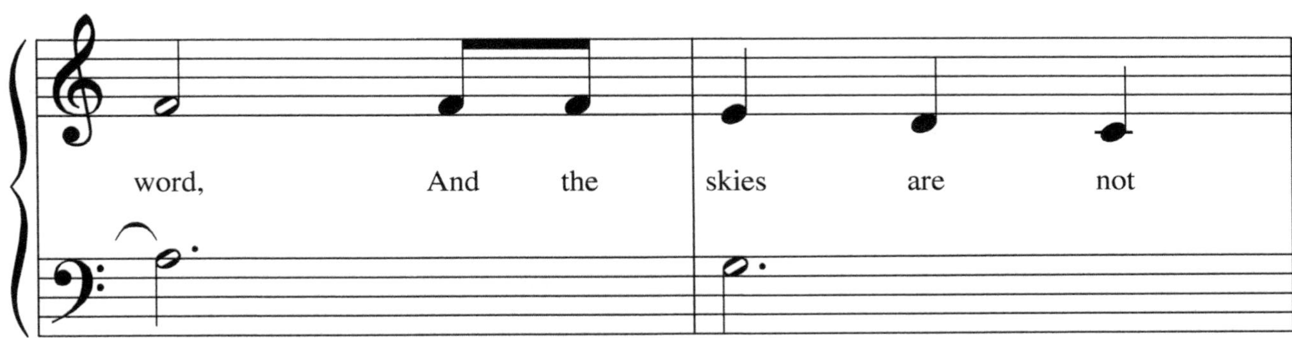
word, And the
skies are not

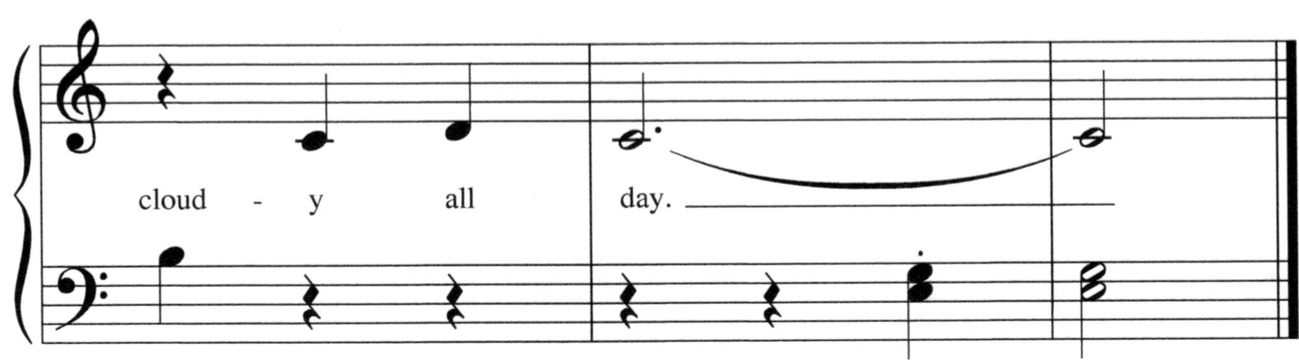
cloud - y all
day.

HUSH, LITTLE BABY

Carolina Folk Lullaby
Arranged by Phillip Keveren

Tenderly
Both hands 8va throughout

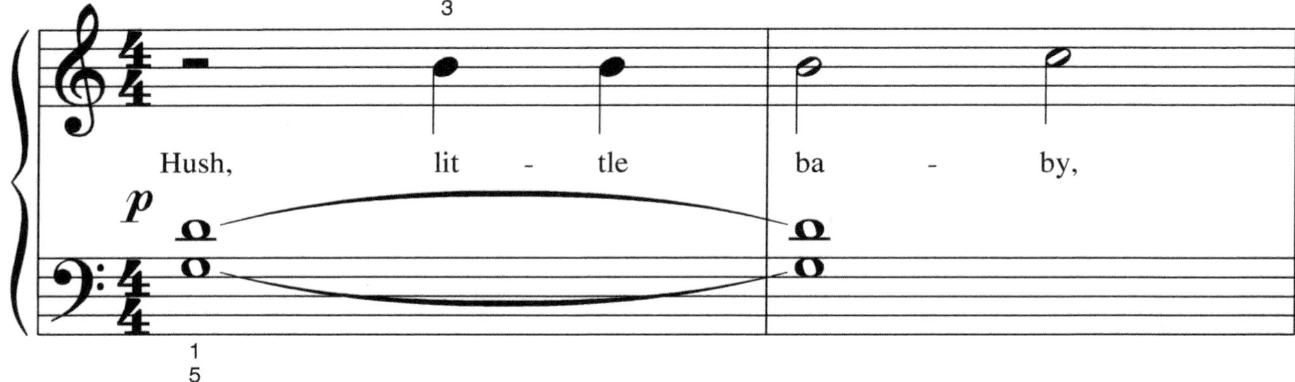

Hold down damper pedal throughout

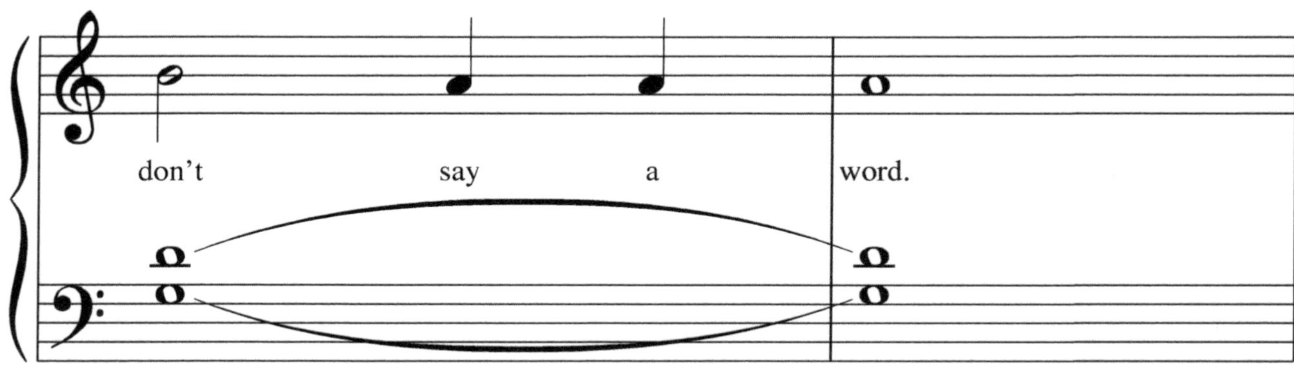

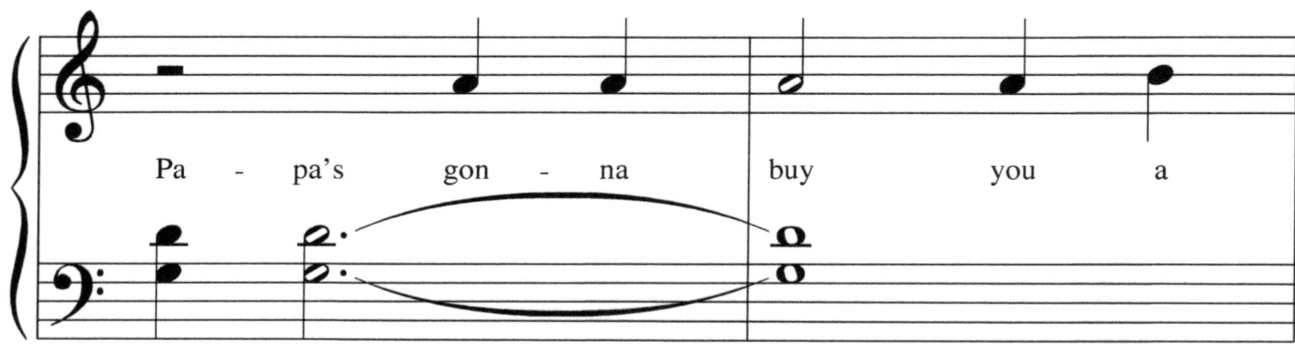

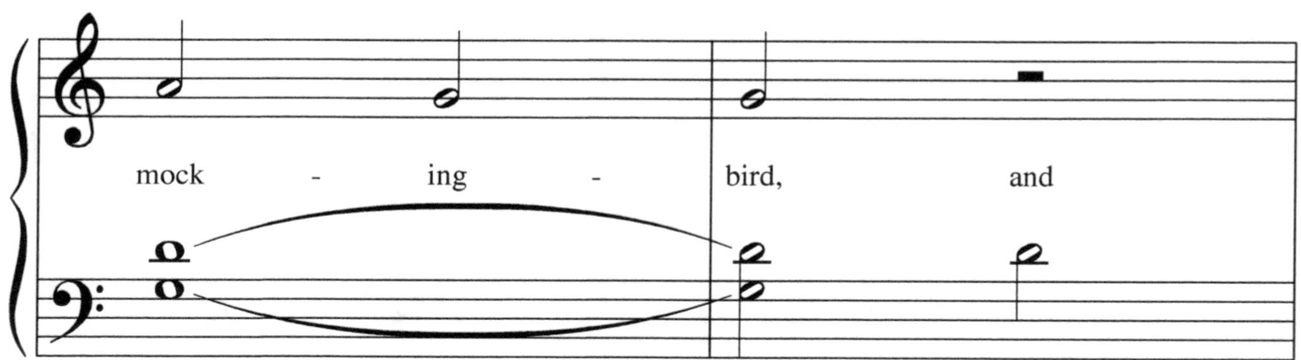

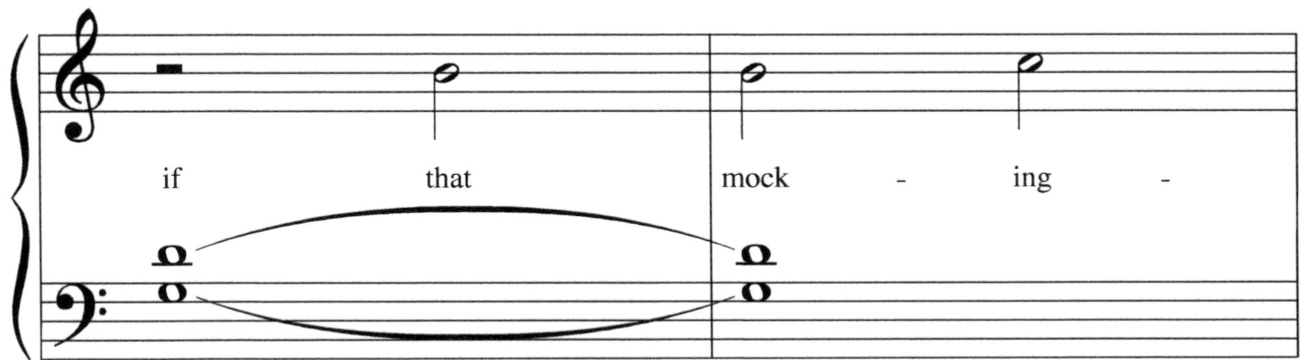
if that mock - ing -

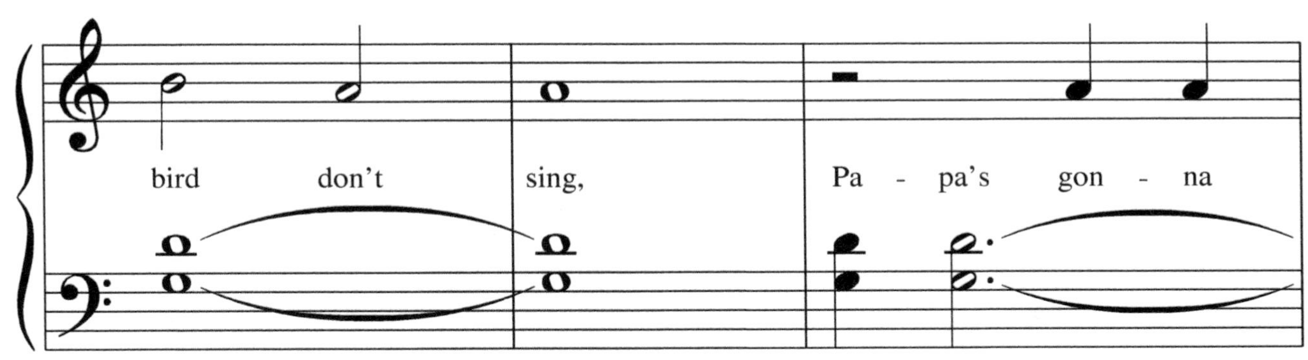
bird don't sing, Pa - pa's gon - na

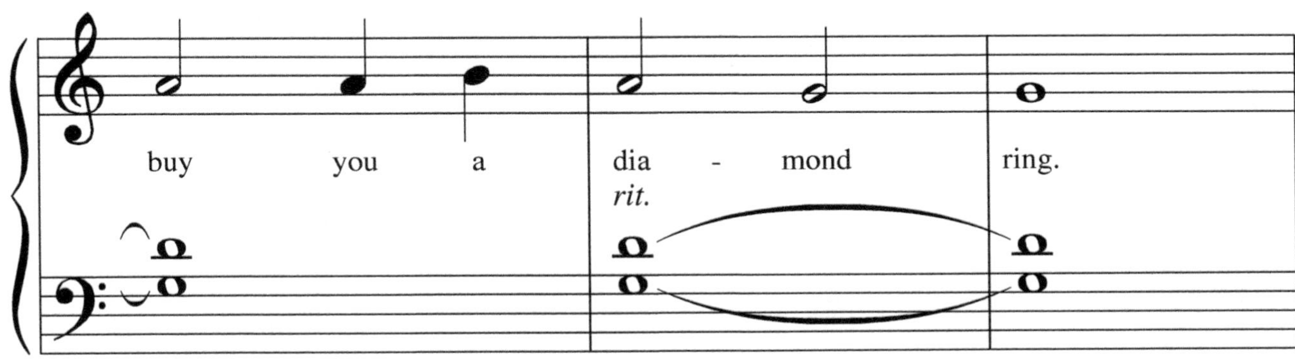
buy you a dia - mond ring.
rit.

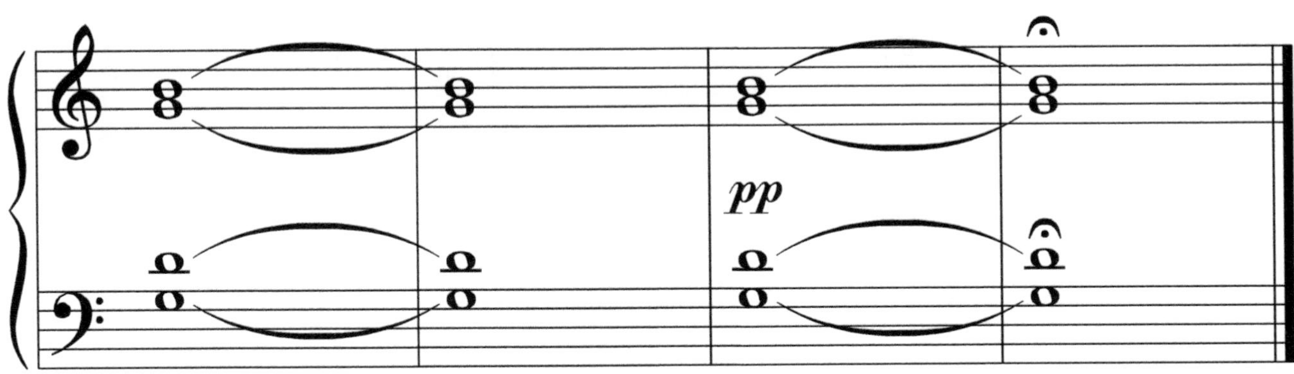
pp

IT'S RAINING, IT'S POURING

Nursery Rhyme Song
Arranged by Phillip Keveren

Drearily

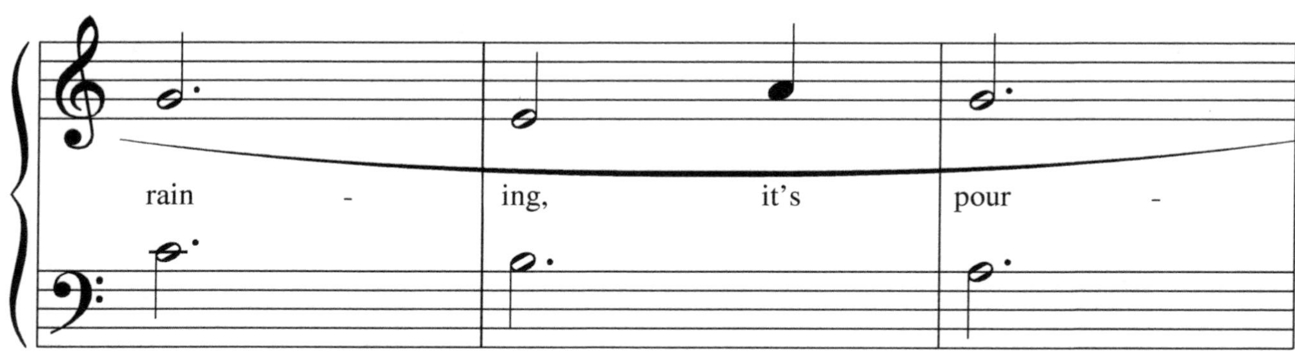

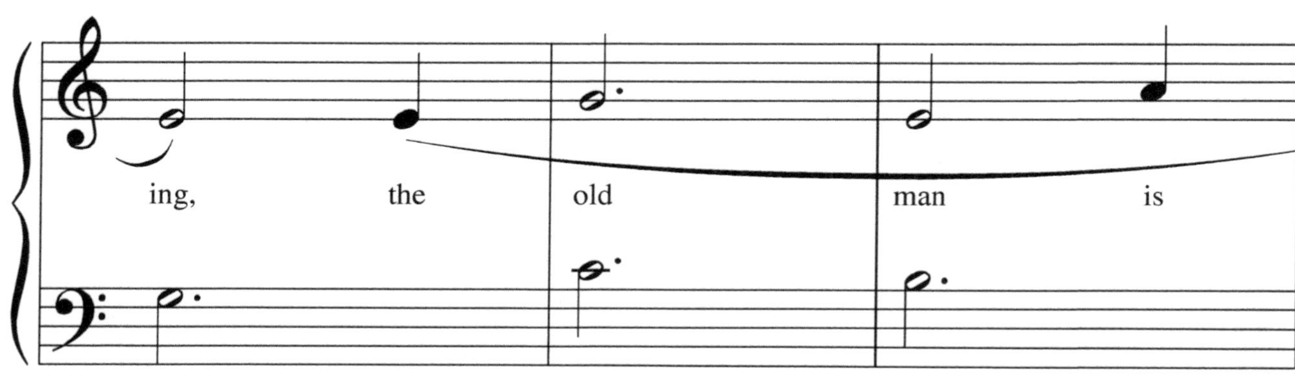

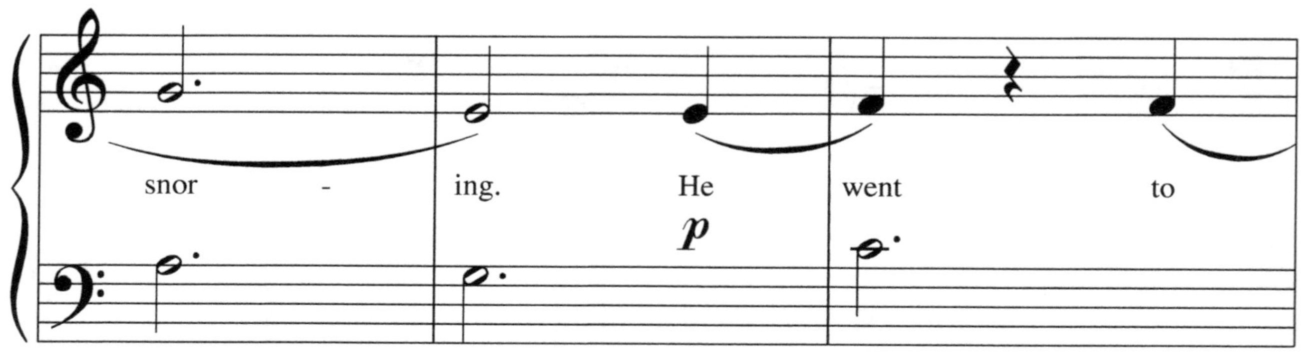

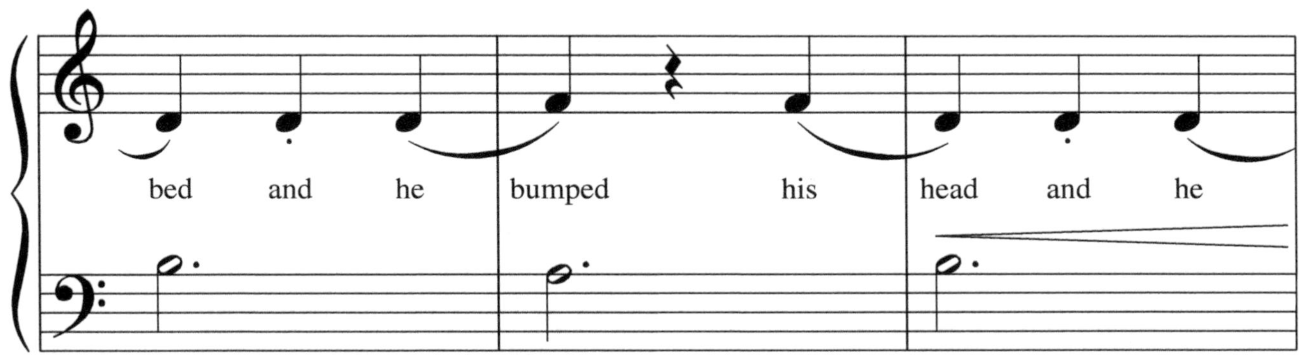
bed and he bumped his head and he

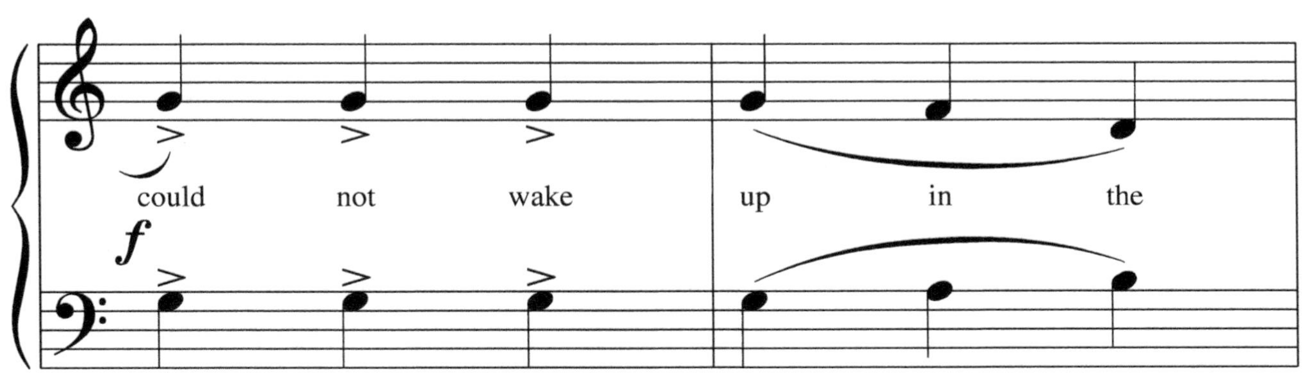
could not wake up in the
f

morn - ing.
4
p
4

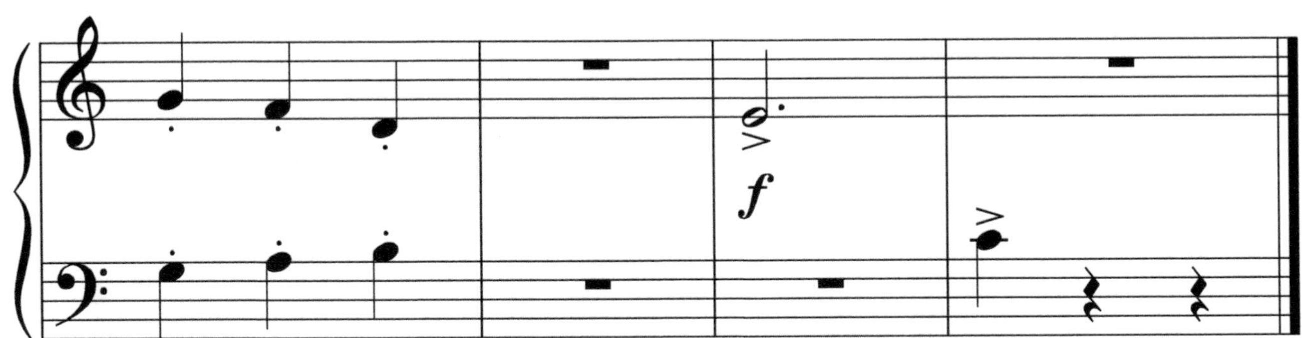
f

LONDON BRIDGE

Nursery Rhyme Song
Arranged by Phillip Keveren

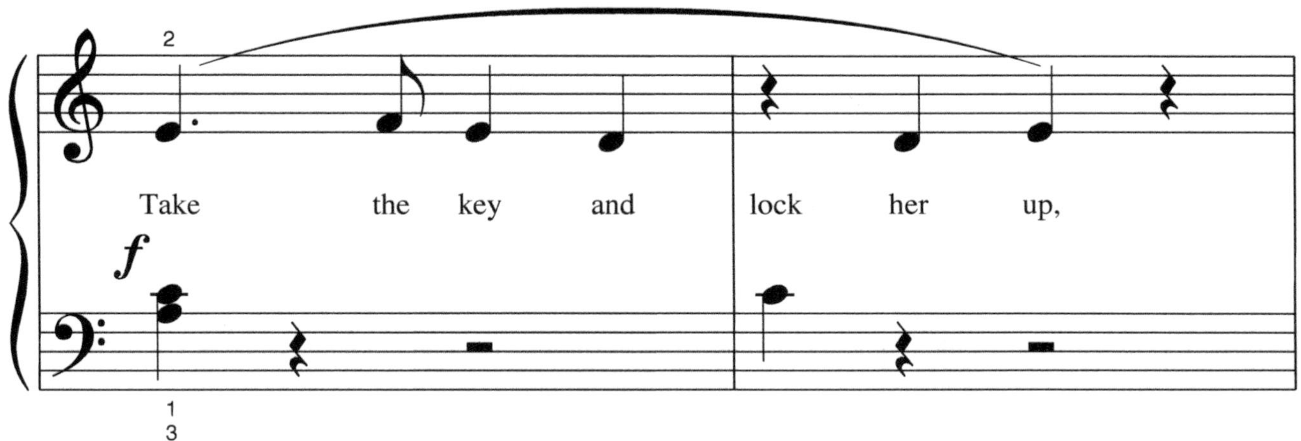
2
Take the key and lock her up,
f
1
3

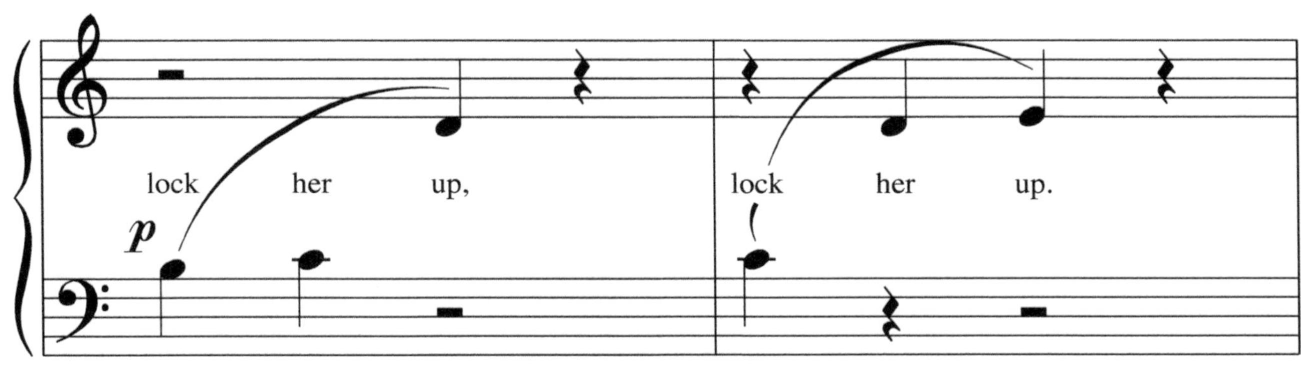
lock her up,
p
lock her up.

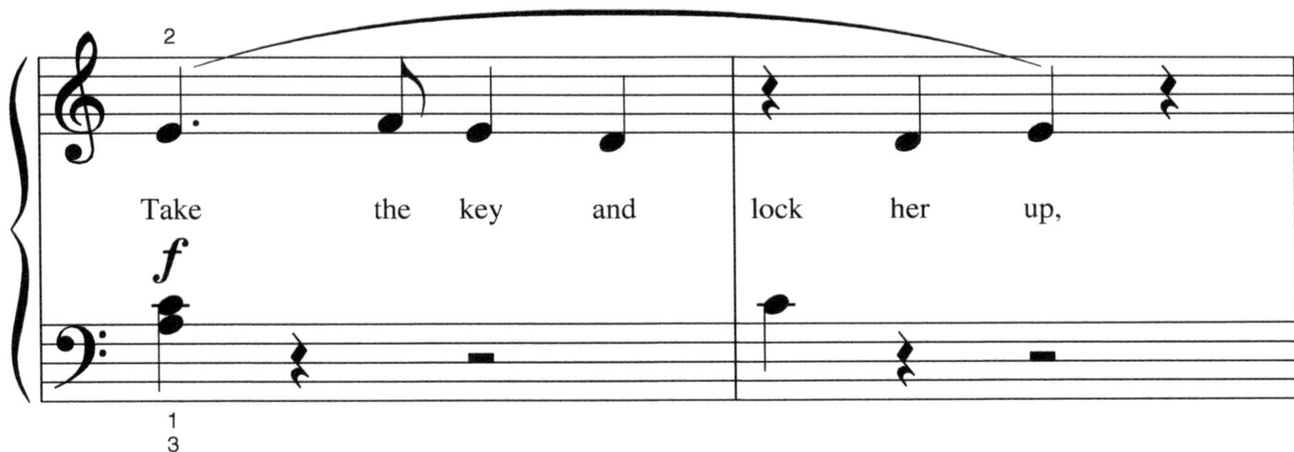
2
Take the key and lock her up,
f
1
3

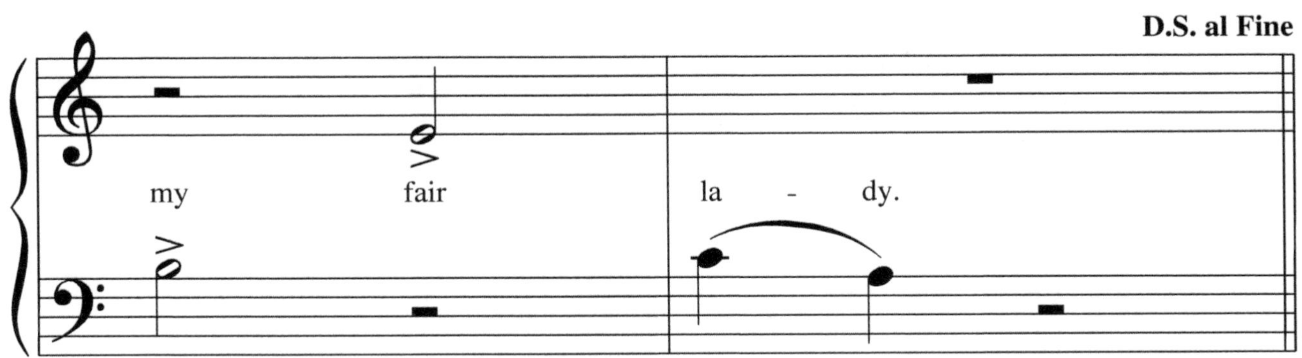
D.S. al Fine
my fair la - dy.

THE MUFFIN MAN

American Folksong
Arranged by Phillip Keveren

MY BONNIE LIES OVER THE OCEAN

Traditional Scottish Folksong
Arranged by Phillip Keveren

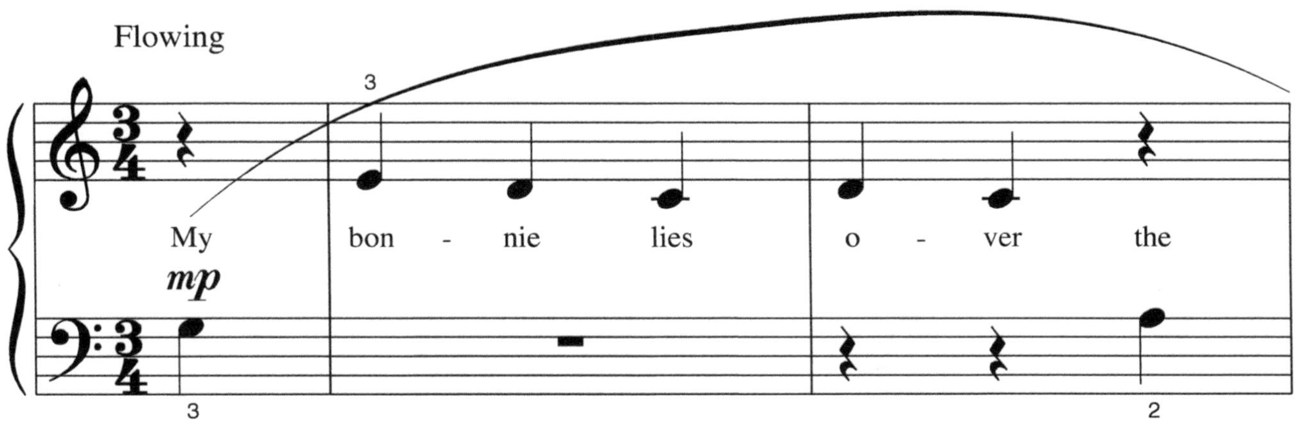

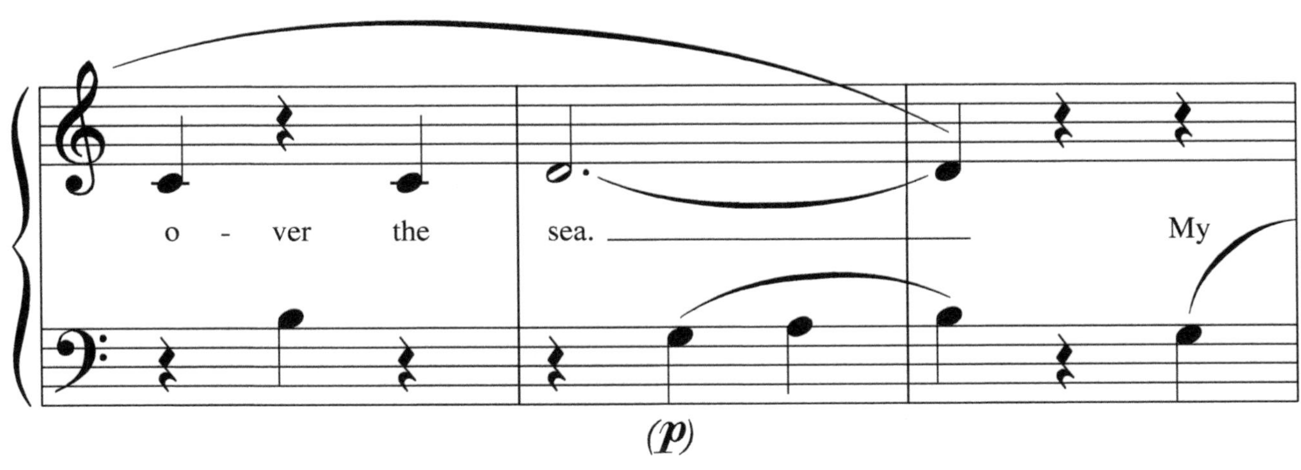

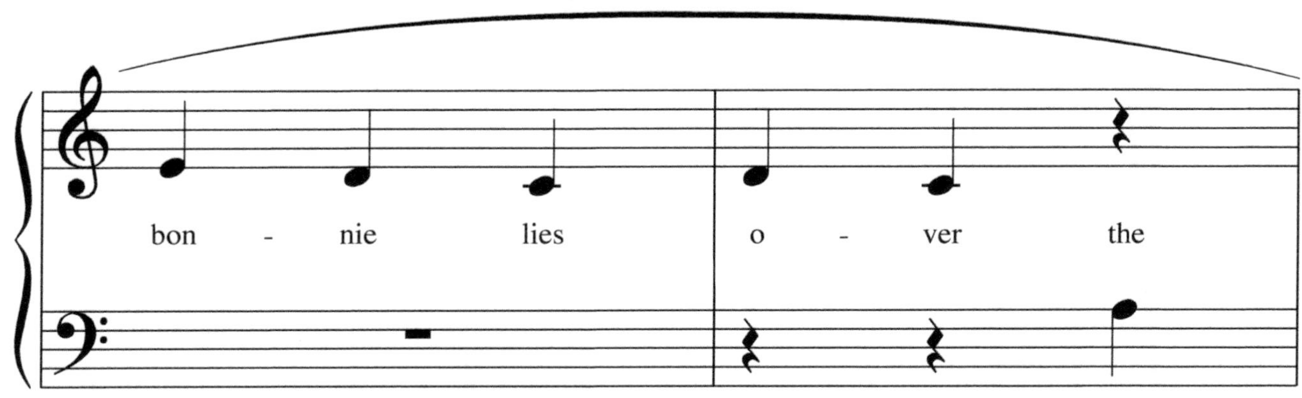
bon - nie lies o - ver the

(p)
o - cean,
Oh bring back my

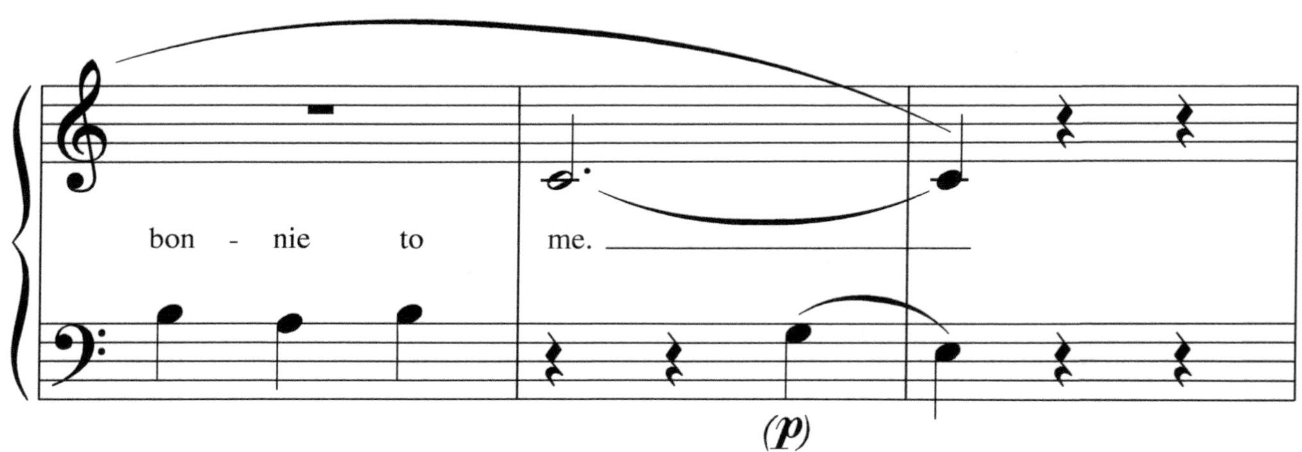
bon - nie to me.
(p)

1
Bring back, bring
mf
3

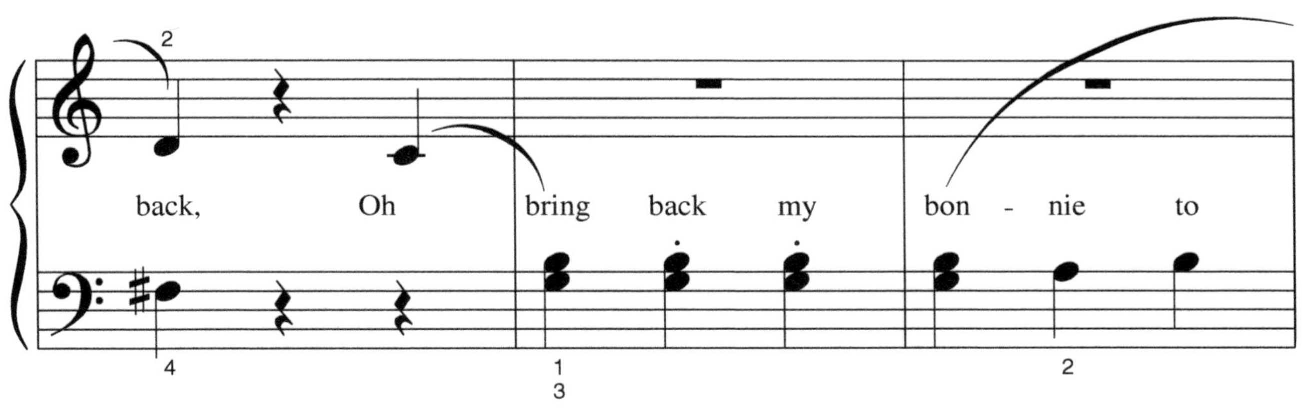
2
back, Oh bring back my bon - nie to
4
1
3
2

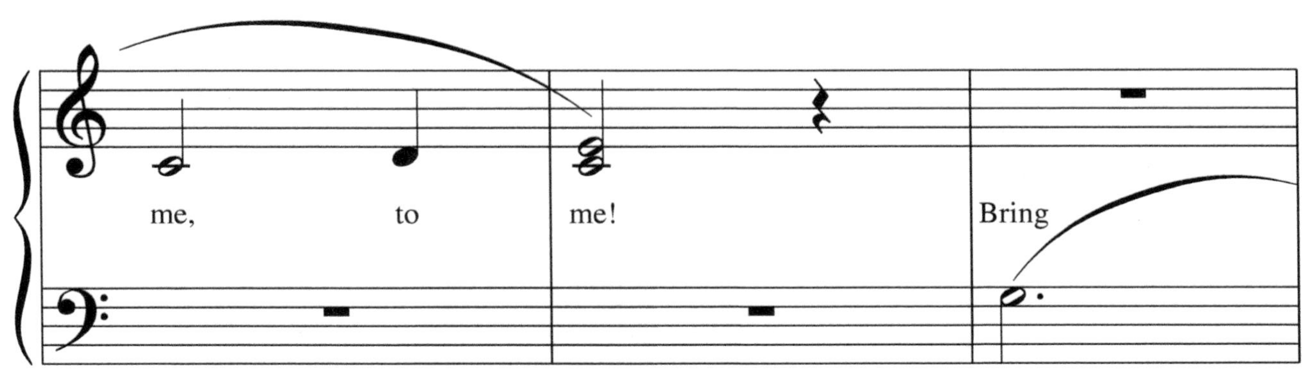
me, to me! Bring

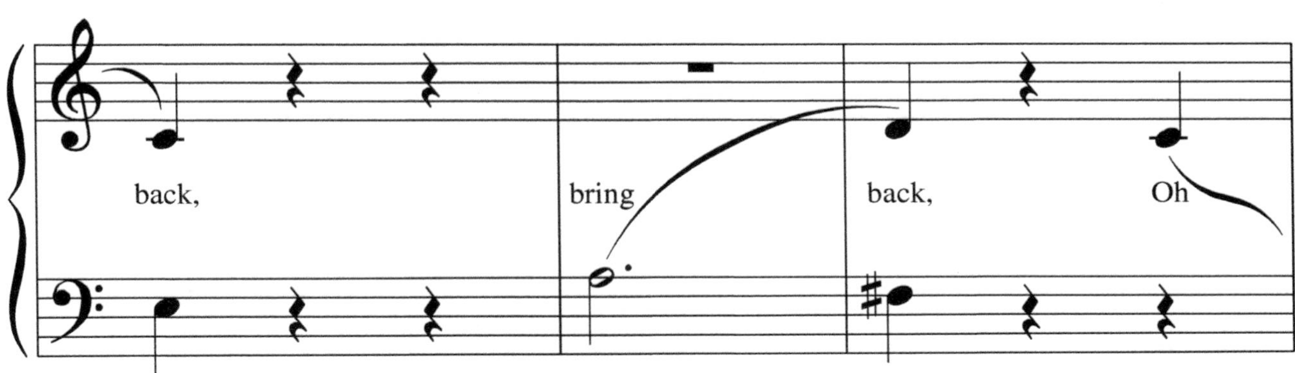
back, bring back, Oh

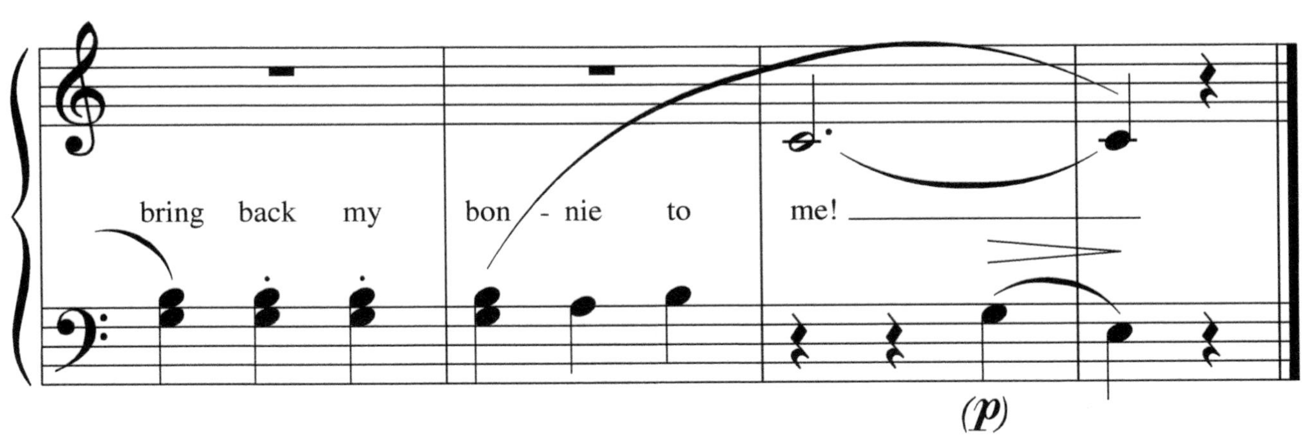
bring back my bon - nie to me!
(p)

OH! SUSANNA

Words and Music by STEPHEN FOSTER
Arranged by Phillip Keveren

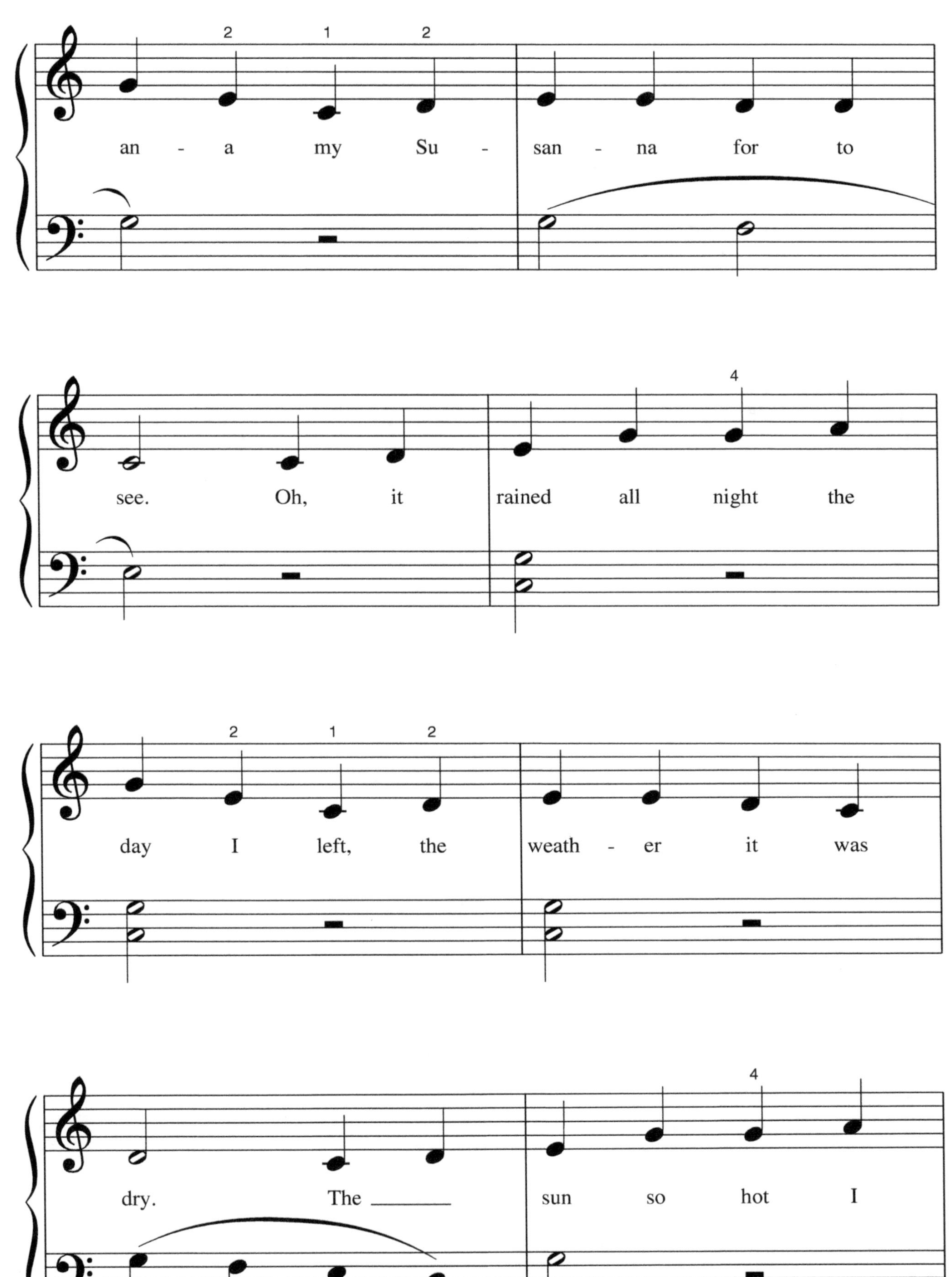
2 1 2
an - a my Su - san - na for to
see. Oh, it rained all night the
4
2 1 2
day I left, the weath - er it was
dry. The sun so hot I
4

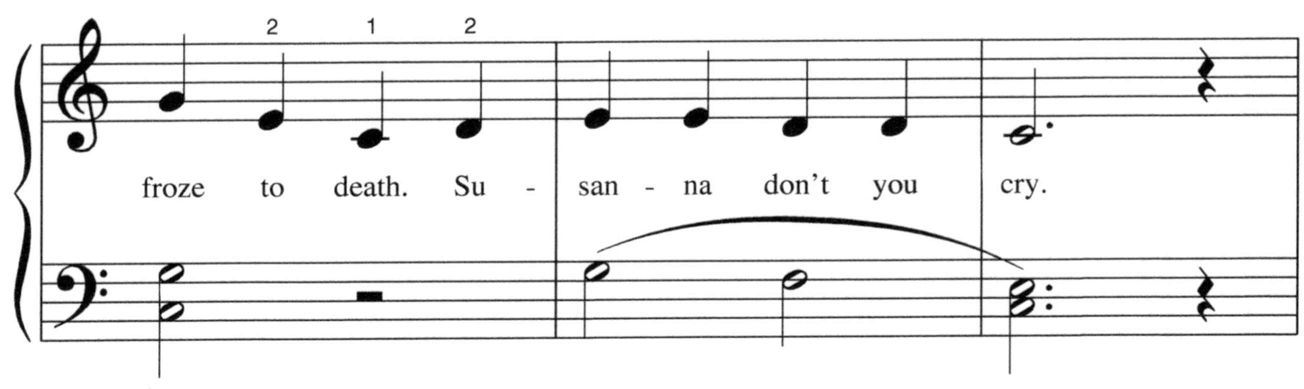
2 1 2
froze to death. Su - san - na don't you cry.

5 4 2 1
Oh, Su - san - na, oh don't you cry for
f
2 1

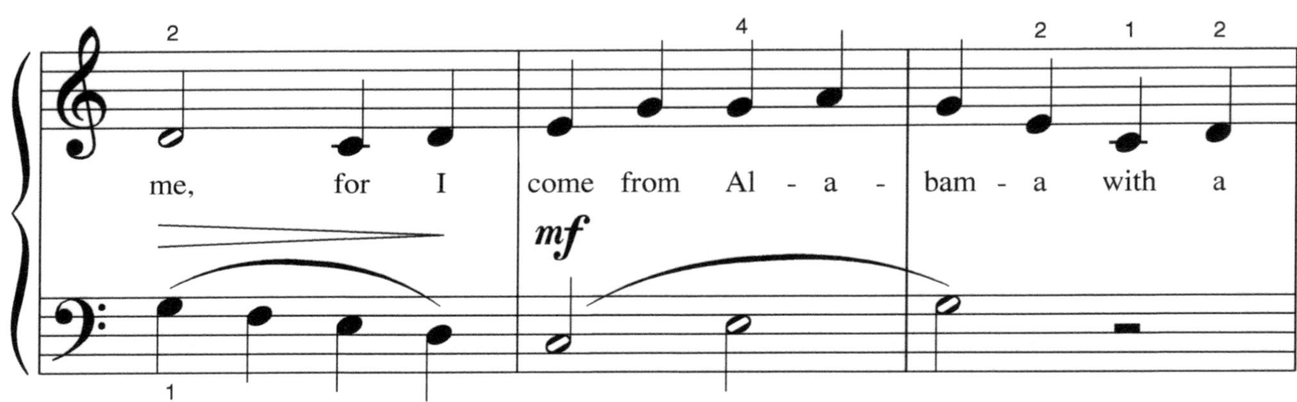
2 4 2 1 2
me, for I come from Al - a - bam - a with a
mf
1

ban - jo on my knee.
f

POP GOES THE WEASEL

Traditional
Arranged by Phillip Keveren

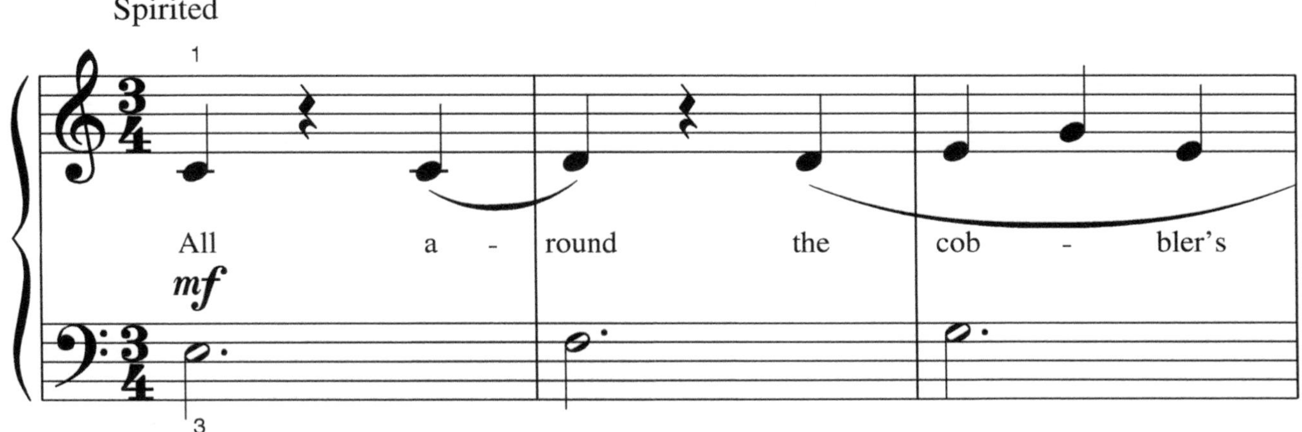

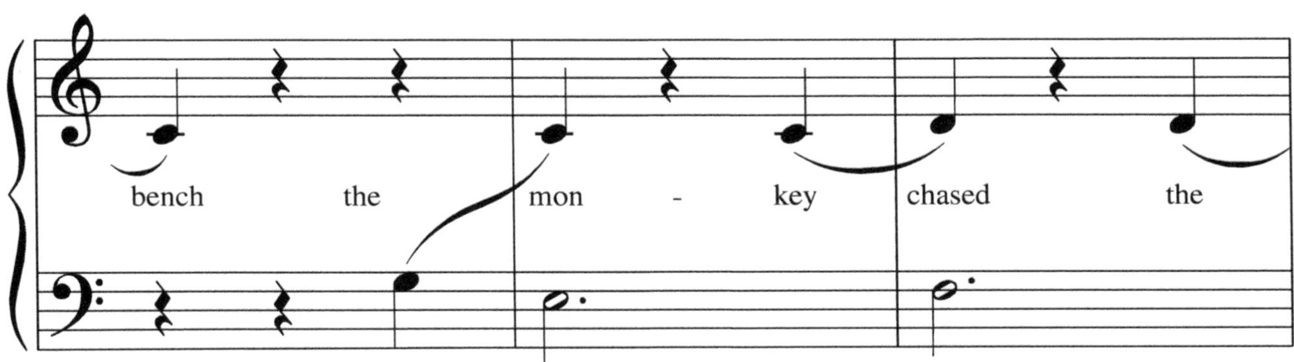

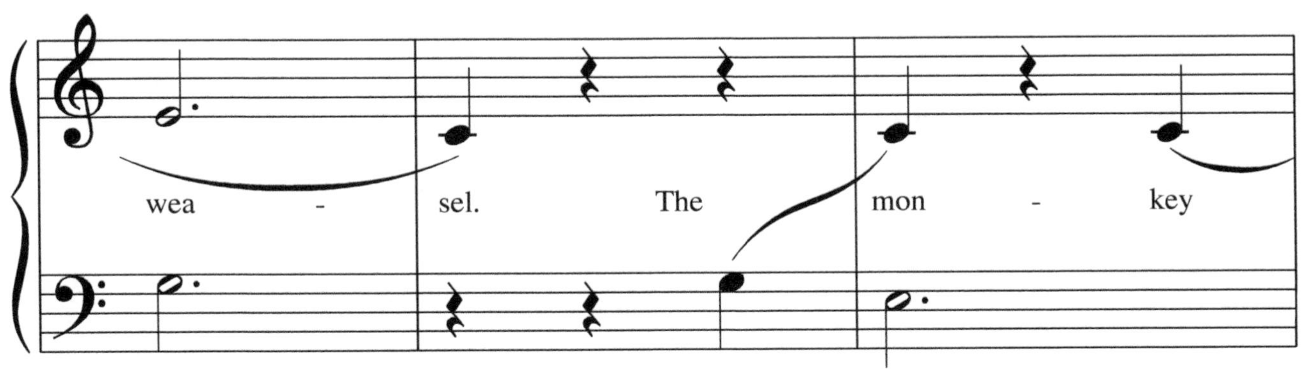

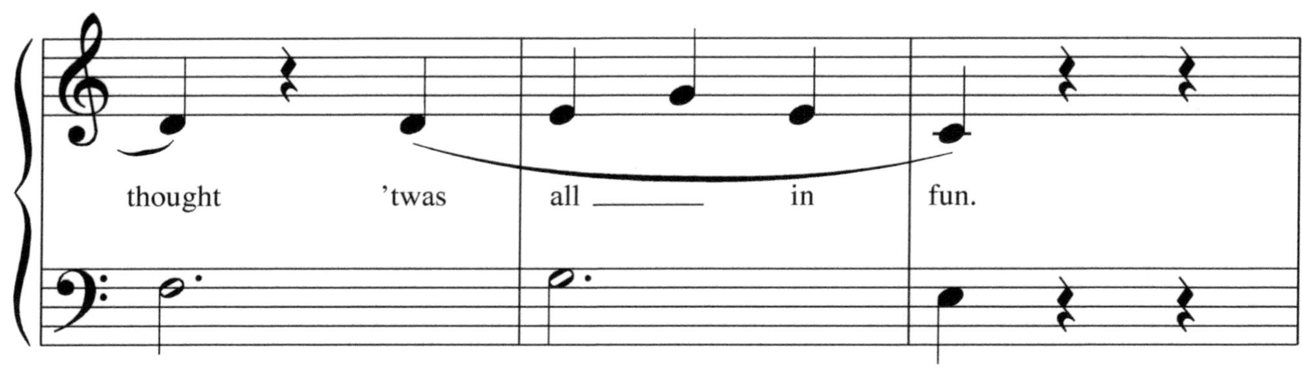
thought 'twas all ___ in fun.

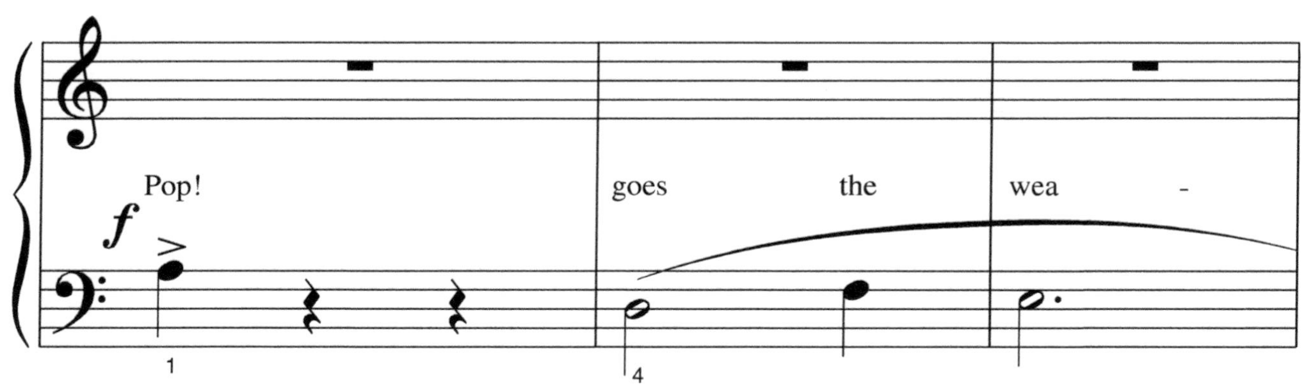
Pop! goes the wea -
f
1
4

1
sel. A pen - ny for a
mp
1

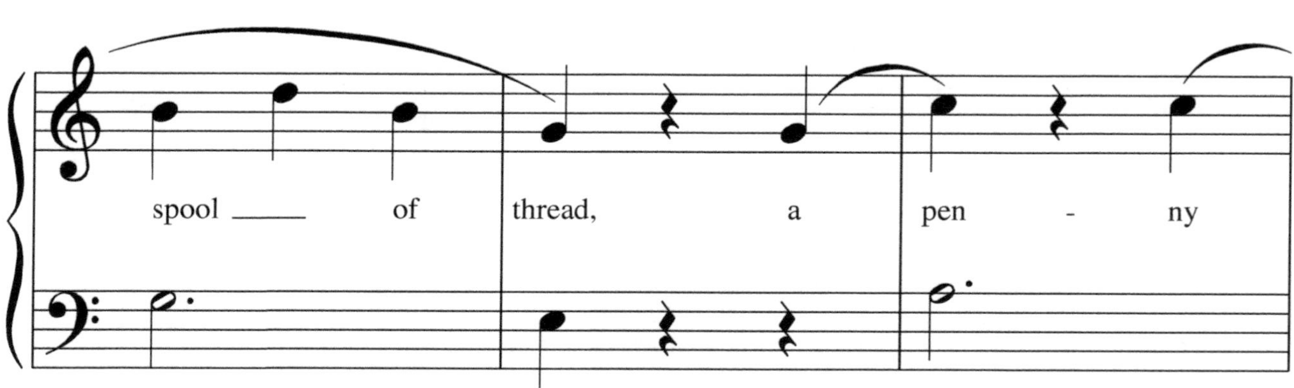
spool ___ of thread, a pen - ny

for
nee - dle.
mf
That's the way the mon - ey
goes.
Pop!
f
goes the
wea - sel.

OH WHERE, OH WHERE HAS MY LITTLE DOG GONE

Words by SEP. WINNER
Traditional Melody
Arranged by Phillip Keveren

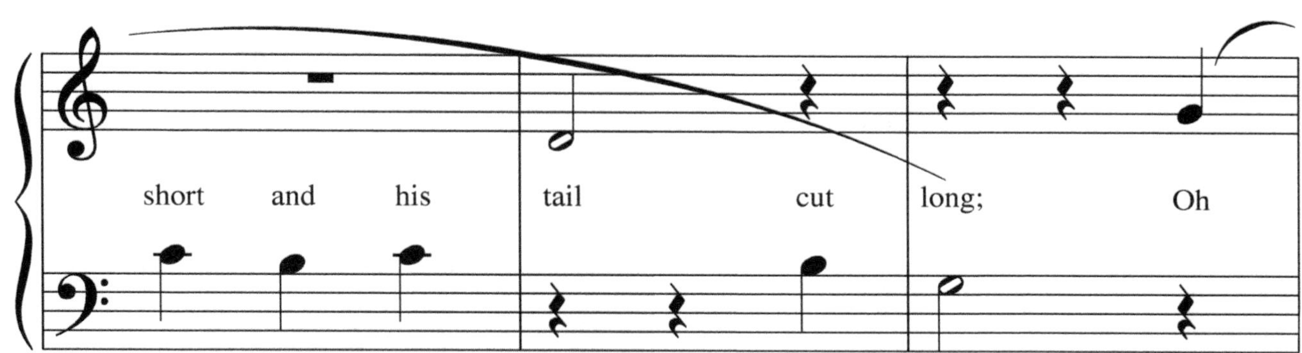
short and his tail cut long; Oh

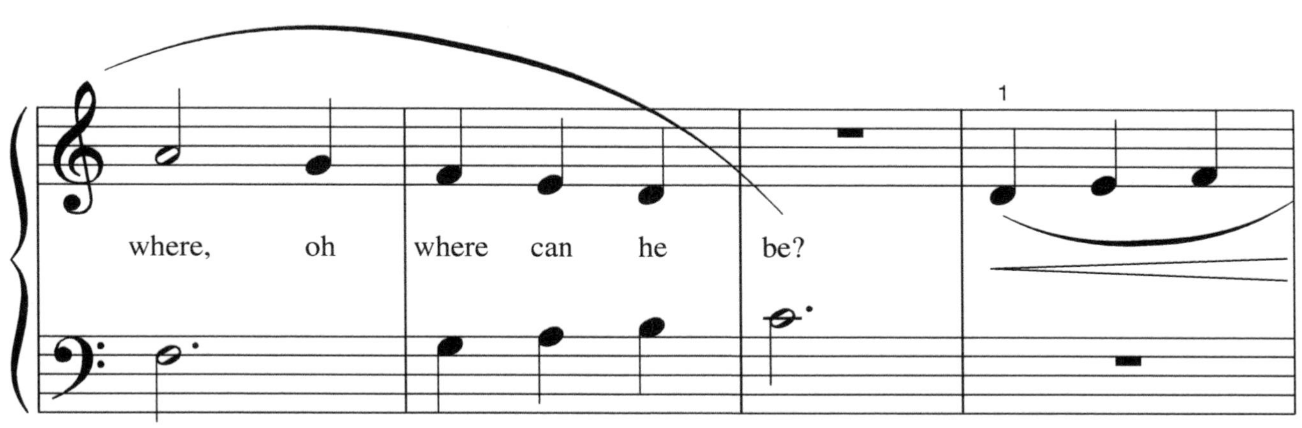
1
where, oh where can he be?

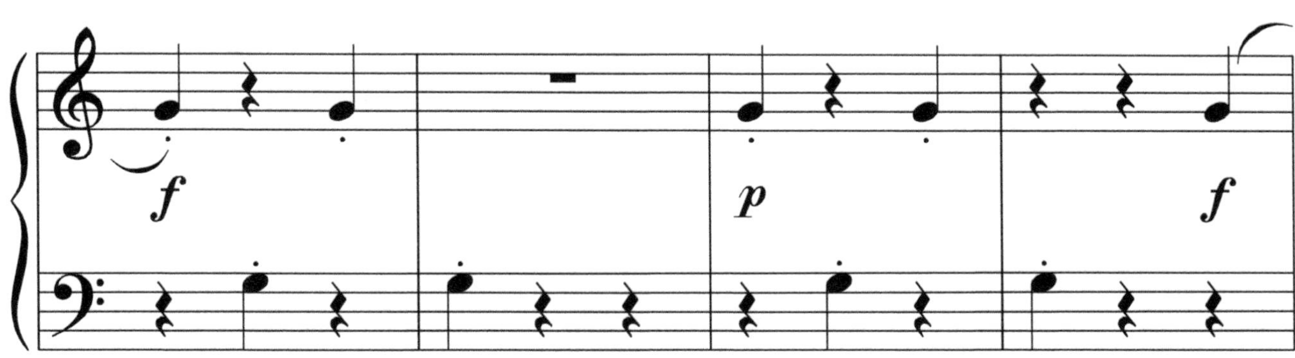
f
p
f

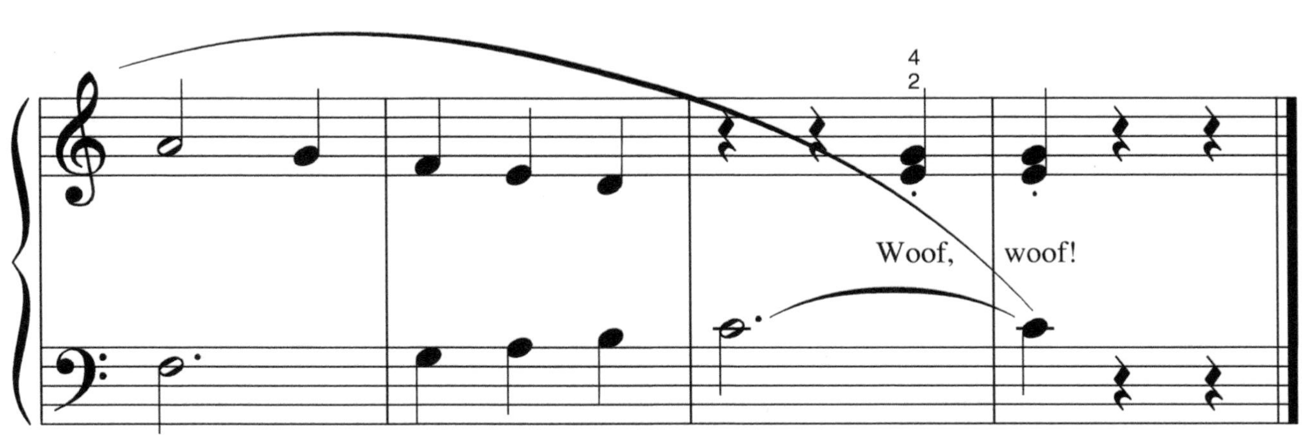
4
2
Woof, woof!

SKIP TO MY LOU

American Game Song
Arranged by Phillip Keveren

Very high chord cluster
(R.H. palm)
Flies in the but - ter - milk. Shoo, shoo, shoo!
p
f
3
3
Flies in the but - ter - milk. Shoo, shoo, shoo!
p
f
Very low chord cluster
(L.H. palm)
Flies in the but - ter - milk. Shoo, shoo, shoo!
p
f
3
2
D.C. al Fine
Skip to my Lou, my dar - lin'.
4

TWINKLE, TWINKLE LITTLE STAR

Traditional
Arranged by Phillip Keveren

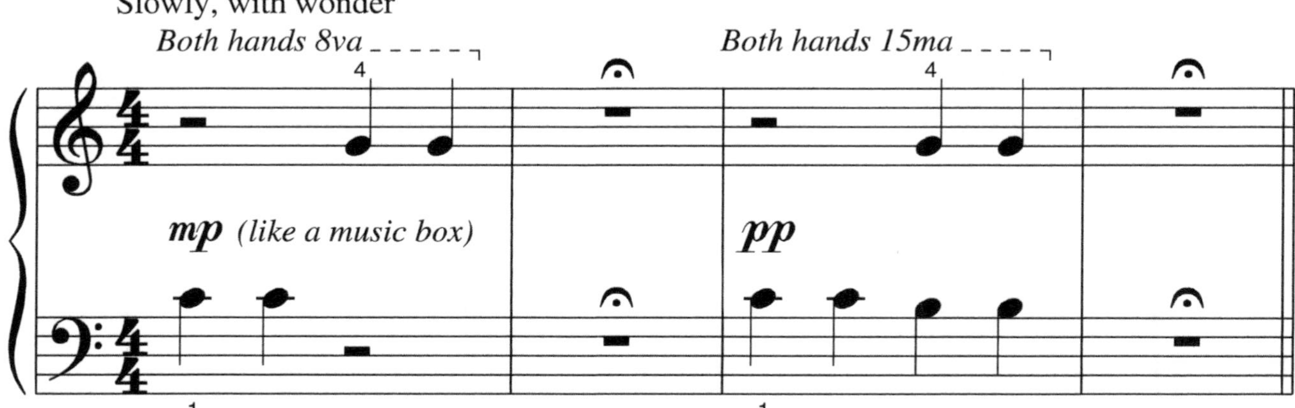

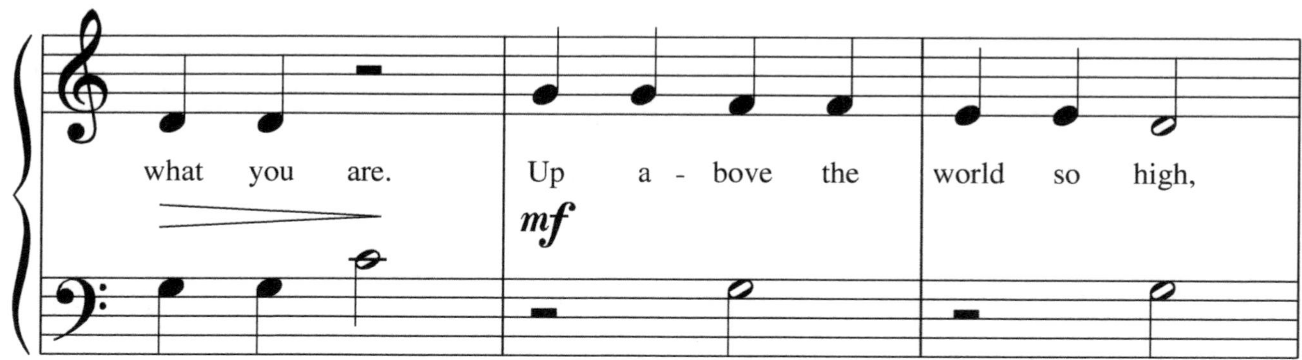

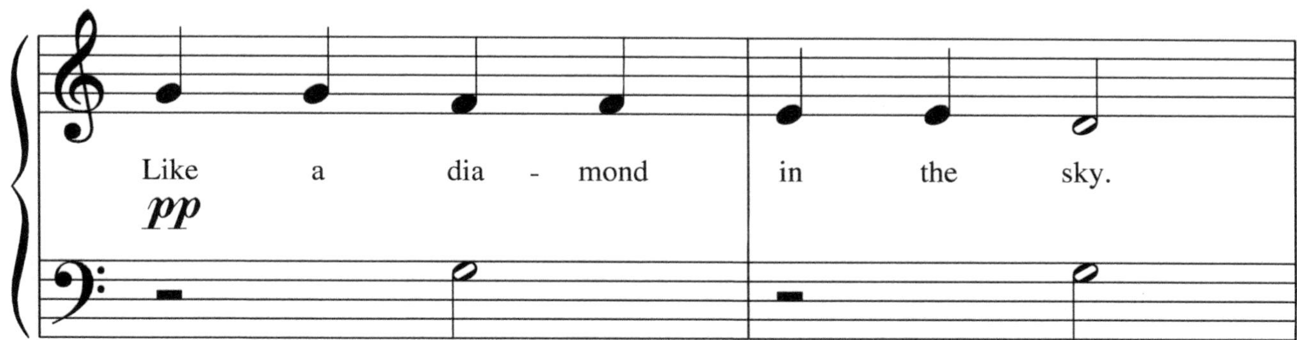
Like a dia - mond in the sky.
pp

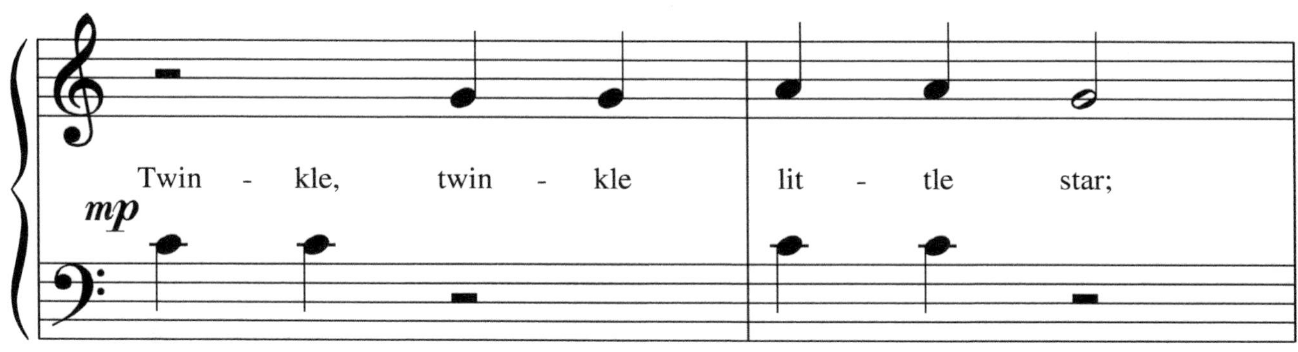
Twin - kle, twin - kle lit - tle star;
mp

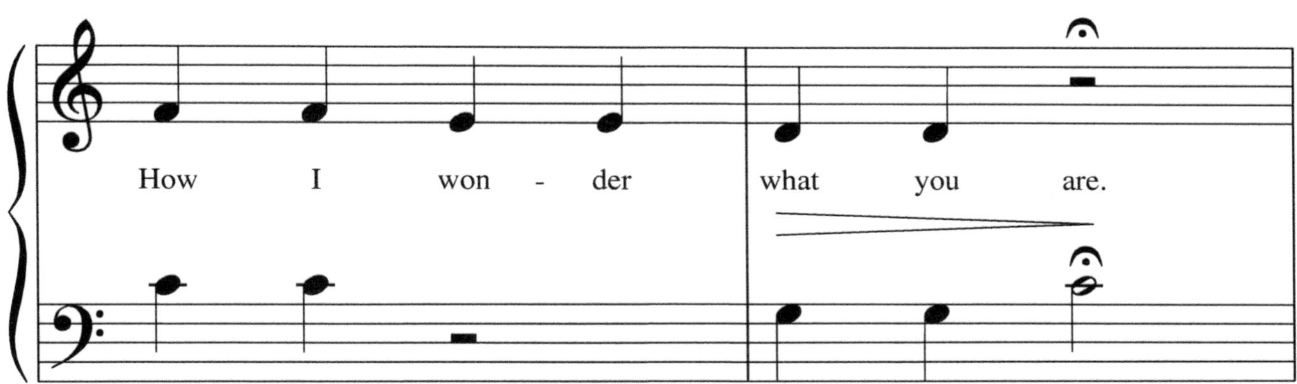
How I won - der what you are.

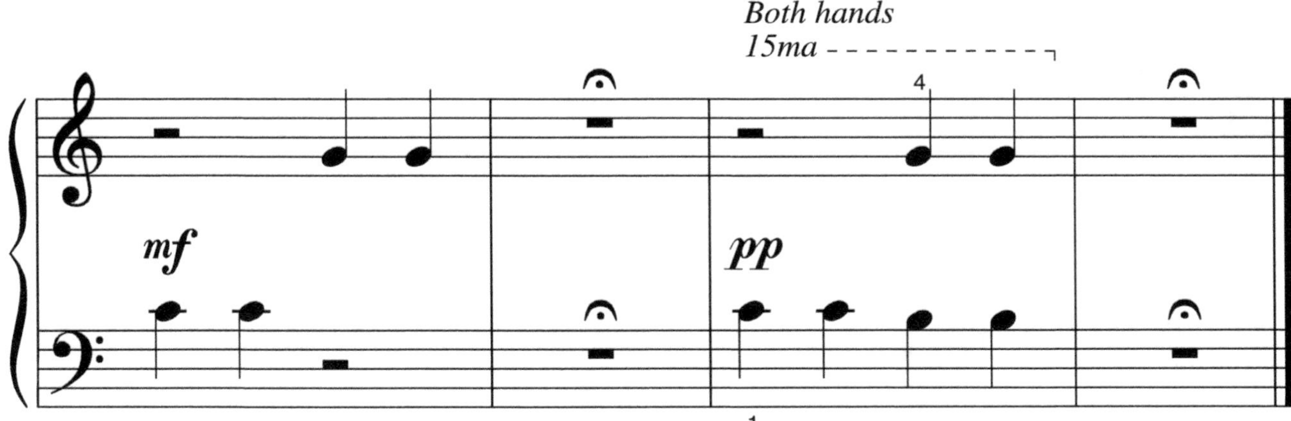
Both hands
15ma
4
mf
pp
1

YANKEE DOODLE

Traditional
Arranged by Phillip Keveren

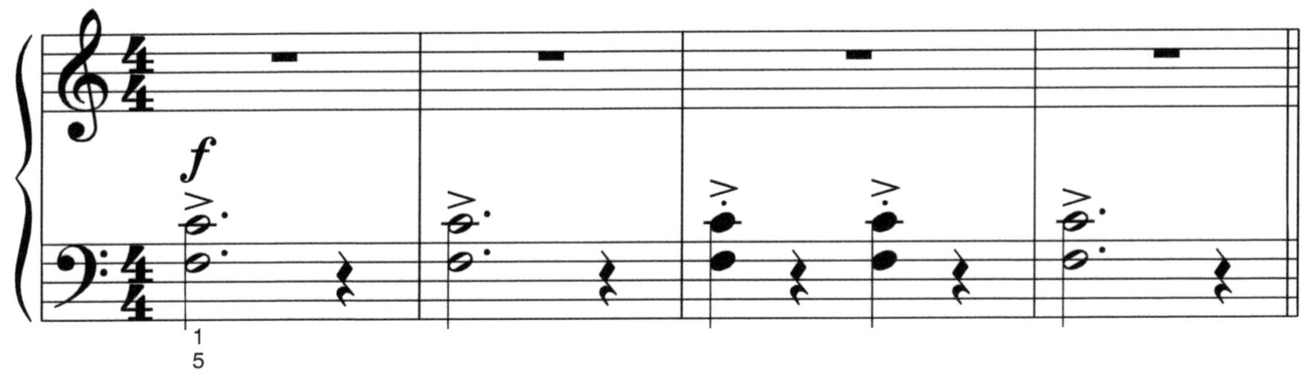

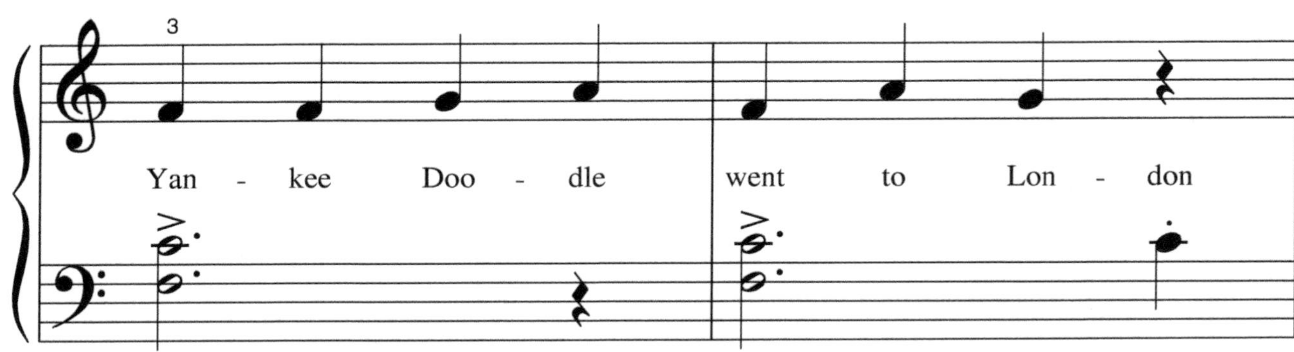

1
Yan - kee Doo - dle,
keep it up;
mp
2
5
1

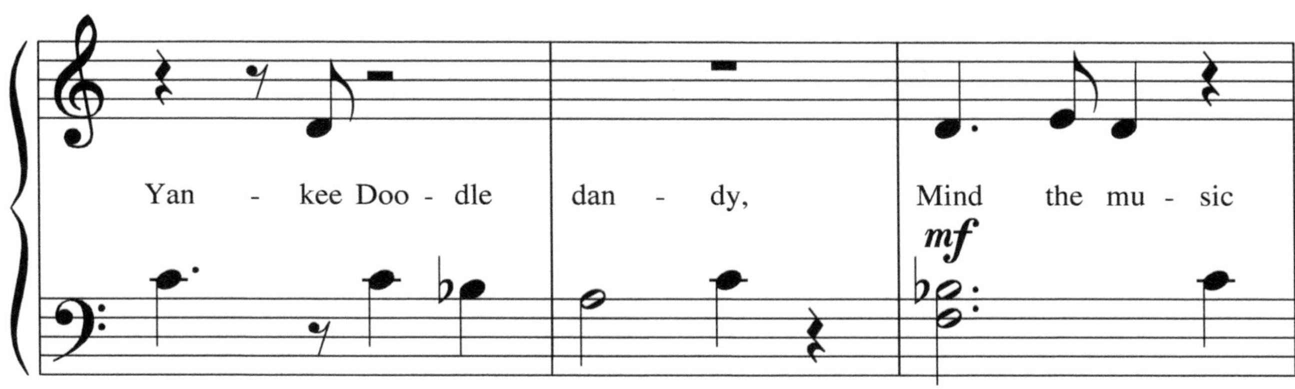
Yan - kee Doo - dle
dan - dy,
Mind the mu - sic
mf

and the step and
with the girls be
han - dy.

f

THREE BLIND MICE

Traditional
Arranged by Phillip Keveren

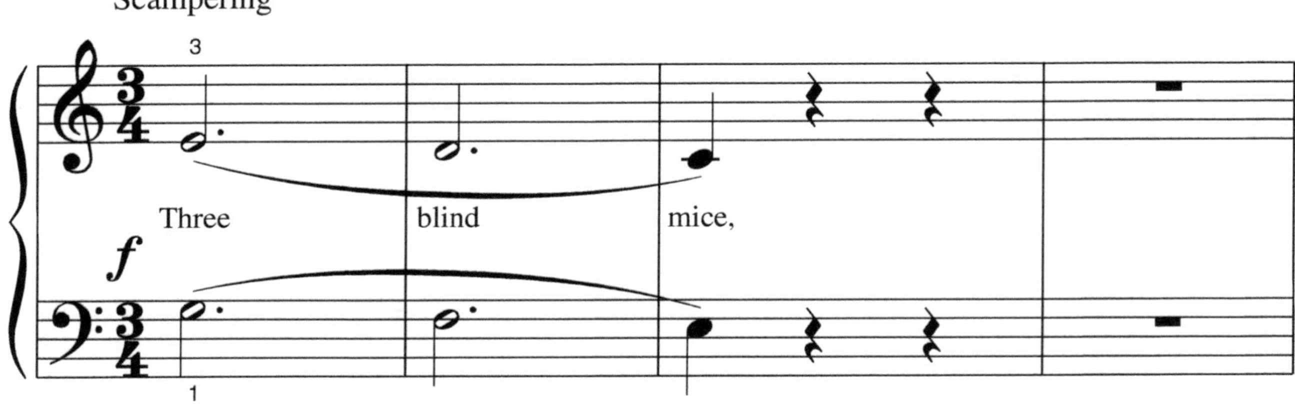

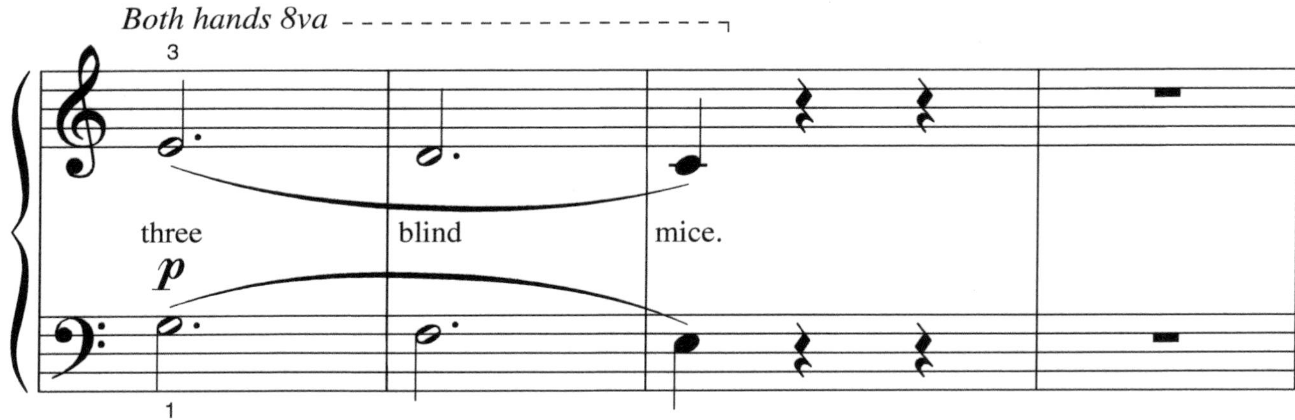

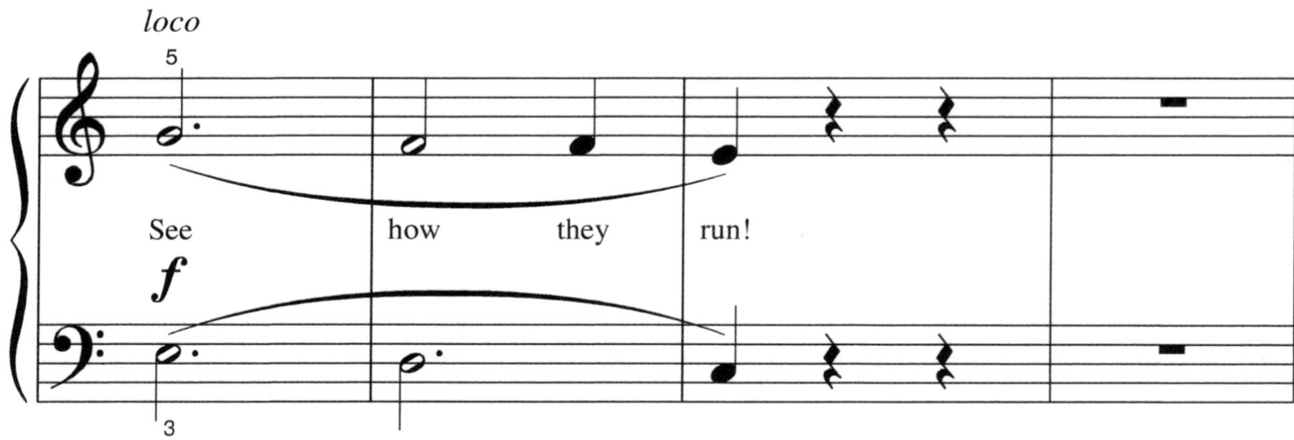

Both hands 8va
See how they run!
p
loco
They all ran af - ter the
mf
farm - er's wife, who cut off their
p
tails with a carv - ing knife. Did
f

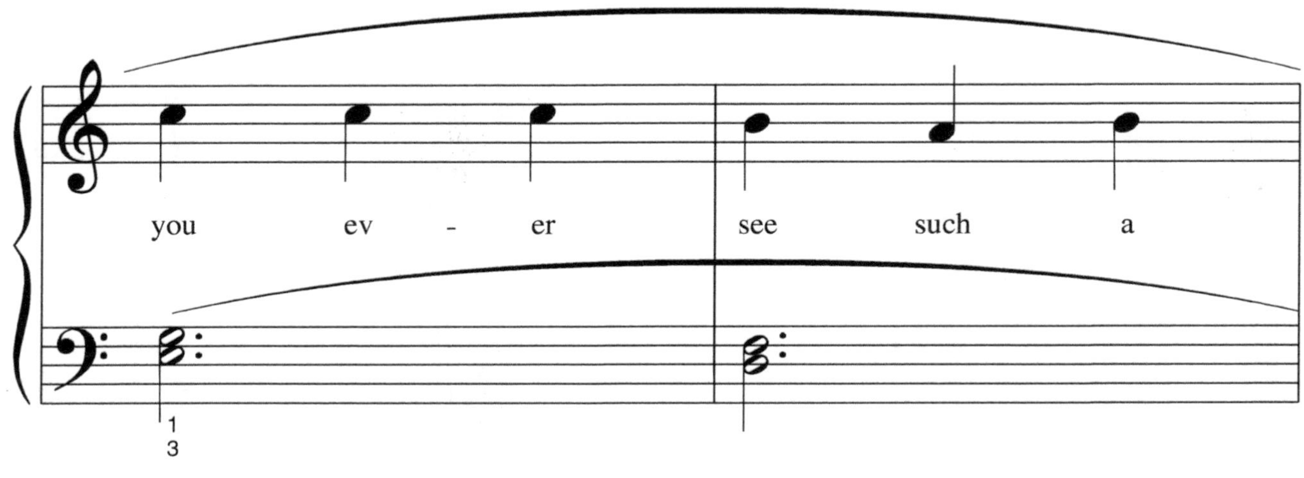
you ev - er see such a
1
3

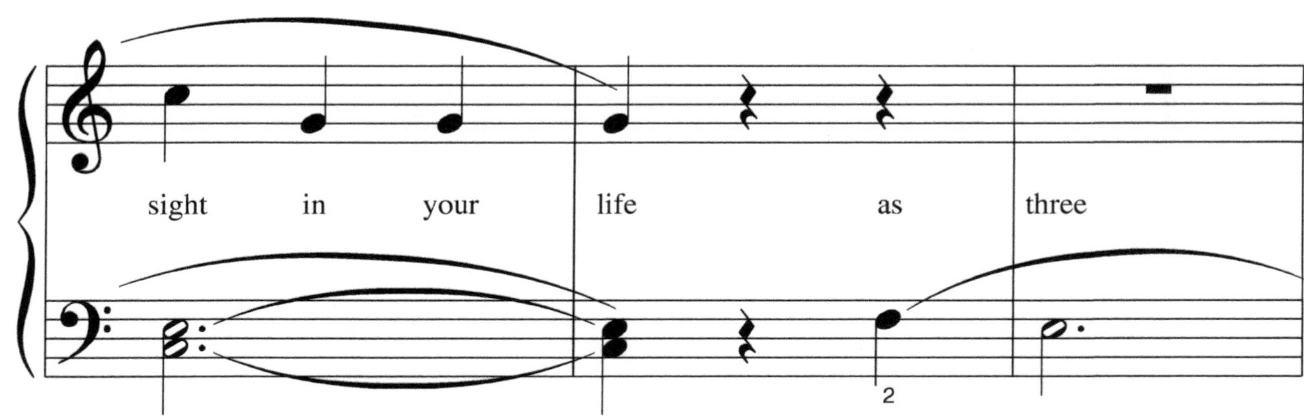
sight in your life as three
2

blind mice.

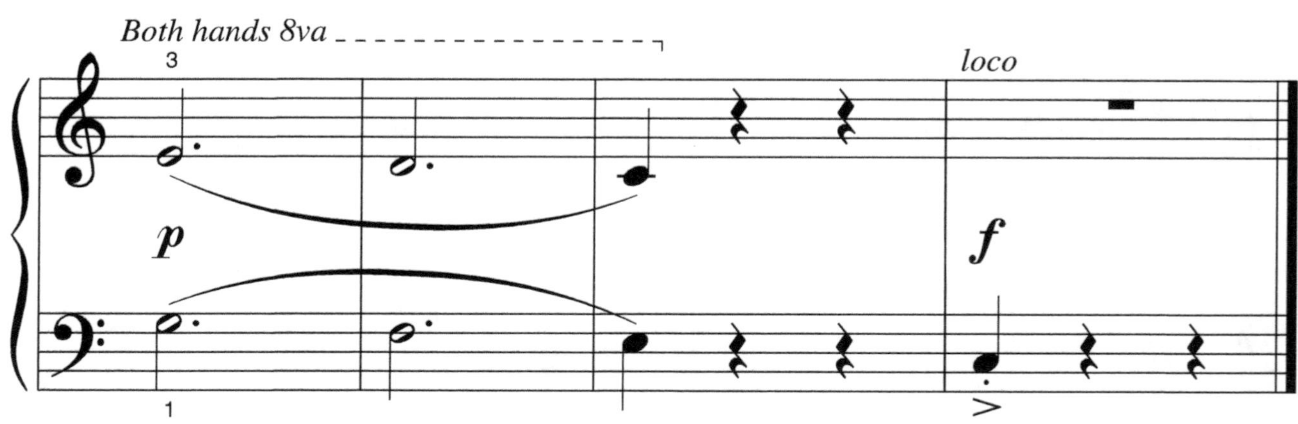
Both hands 8va
3
loco
p
f
1